Legal Lore
Curiosities of Law and Lawyers

Legal Lore

Curiosities of Law and Lawyers

edited by William Andrews

BeardBooks
Washington, D.C.

London: William Andrews & Co., 1897
Reprinted 2001 by Beard Books, Washington, D.C.
ISBN 1-58798-102-5

Printed in the United States of America

TRIAL OF A PIG AT LAUSANNE IN THE FOURTEENTH CENTURY.

Preface.

THE favourable reception given to my volume issued under the title of "The Lawyer in History, Literature, and Humour," has induced me to prepare, on similar lines, the present book, dealing with curiosities of the law. I hope those who are interested in the study of the byways of literature may find entertainment and instruction in its pages, and that it will win a welcome not only from the legal profession, but from the reading public.

I am enabled by the courtesy of Messrs. Chatto & Windus, to reproduce for my frontispiece, an illustration from a work published by them, under the title of "Credulities Past and Present."

WILLIAM ANDREWS.

THE HULL PRESS,
    10th December, 1896.

Contents.

	PAGE
BIBLE LAW. By S. Burgess, M.A.	1
SANCTUARIES. By William E. A. Axon, F.R.S.L.	13
TRIALS IN SUPERSTITIOUS AGES. By Ernest H. Rann	23
ON SYMBOLS. By George Neilson	43
LAW UNDER THE FEUDAL SYSTEM. By Cuming Walters	58
THE MANOR AND MANOR LAW. By England Howlett	83
ANCIENT TENURES. By England Howlett	95
LAWS OF THE FOREST. By Edward Peacock, F.S.A.	109
TRIAL BY JURY IN OLD TIMES. By Thomas Frost	122
BARBAROUS PUNISHMENTS. By Sidney W. Clarke	132
TRIALS OF ANIMALS. By Thomas Frost	149
DEVICES OF THE SIXTEENTH CENTURY DEBTORS. By James C. Macdonald, F.S.A., Scot.	161
LAWS RELATING TO THE GIPSIES. By William E. A. Axon, F.R.S.L.	165
COMMONWEALTH LAW AND LAWYERS. By Edward Peacock F.S.A.	179
COCK-FIGHTING IN SCOTLAND.	197
COCKIELEERIE LAW. By Robert Bird	200
FATAL LINKS. By Ernest H. Rann	205
POST-MORTEM TRIALS. By George Neilson	224
ISLAND LAWS. By Cuming Walters	237
THE LITTLE INNS OF COURT.	258
OBITER. By George Neilson	267
INDEX	277

LEGAL LORE.

Bible Law.

By S. Burgess, m.a.

AT the very outset of any treatment of so delicate a subject as that indicated by the title of this chapter, we are met by no small difficulty. This consists in the danger of committing unintentional errors of irreverence, and thus offending the prejudices of those who are more or less pledged to their belief in the verbal inspiration of every Bible chapter and verse. With this risk before us, we can only trust to our own sense of a rational view of a subject so full of capabilities of misconstruction. Those of us who can remember the outburst of righteous indignation at the publication of the " Essays and Reviews " and of " Ecce Homo," feel surprise at the quiet indifference with which views expressed in them are now received. This does not at all, or necessarily, mean that men's faith is colder, or that the spirit of reverent religious feelings has died away. The advance of accurate scientific investigation may have upset the faith of some, and given a subject for outbursts of intolerant pulpit denunciations, but we must think that there are signs plainly discernible of a quiet acceptation of modern discovery by the majority of thoughtful and devout believers in the inspiration of Holy Scripture. These remarks will be found not unneedful as we pursue the examination of this particular branch of Biblical study, namely, the Law as it is found in the Bible, and this will be seen at once when it is laid down as an absolutely necessary condition of our investigation that this same Law can plainly be divided into two distinct portions—that which is of Divine, and that which is of human origin. The bare statement of this fact will offend certain prejudices. The Divine "Fiat" stamps with as marvellous and undoubted clearness, certain portions, as other parts are marked by the progress of human intelligence, the needs of human society, and the force of the human will.

The very fact of the existence of Law entails the necessity of Penalty, and this may be spiritual or corporal. The former depends on the acknowledgment of the rule over us of a Superior Being. The latter is a necessary accompaniment of all and every human life, believing or unbelieving. So in the Bible Law we can easily distinguish between the penalty affixed to the breaking of the first of the Ten Commandments, and that which followed on the breaking of the sixth. On the authority of Hebrew scholars, we are told that the use of the Hebrew Article shows that *The Law* refers to the expressed will of God. If this rule be invariable, it would be of great value, and especially so in the use of the Greek Article.

The writers of the Psalms gave forth an intense reflection of the old Law; always presuming, as they of course did, that it emanated from the Deity.

Now let us be allowed to start with the assumption that the Mosaic is the earliest form of tabulated Law. A most excellent book has just been published, "The History of Babylonia," by the Society for Promoting Christian Knowledge. It is a cheap little book, but full of information upon which one feels able to rely. We find there that the Moral Law of Babylonia represents the spirit of Bible Law so accurately that it would be absurd to set up any theory of an independent basis.

We must make a date somewhere, and therefore we cannot do better than choose a date that can be fairly tested, and safely on this side of mythical eras,—and that is about 1500 B.C. This must appear a very safe and modest date to fall back upon. The Babylonians want us to go back 432,000 years, but to accept this assertion requires more faith than most of us possess.

For our present purpose there is nothing gained by comparing the Mosaic Law with that discovered with such infinite care and learning in the Babylonian records. The utmost that can be said is that we have startling coincidences, and an intensely interesting subject opened out. But there is no single grain of information, and that is what we are just now in search of. We feel quite distrustful of documents, especially *stone* ones, which give the lifetime of Alorus as extending to 36,000 years. That was before the Deluge. The Wandering Jew sinks into insignificance, and is a mere puling infant by the side of such figures as these, because the son of Alorus reigned for

46,800 years. However short the "year" was, the period of life was quite lengthy. If a year was our week, the last named patriarch was about 1,000 years old.

This is a departure somewhat from the Law as it is in our Bibles. But it will be an interesting study for some kind student to compare that Law with the echoes thereof found in Asiatic literature, even far away on the eastern shores of China. The mystery still unsolved is, "*How did it get there?*"

With the greatest diffidence we make the statement that the first notion of Law was in connection with sacrifice. The time may come when this can be refuted. But at present, leaving out of the question natural and unwritten Law, we find no bond but this. Sacrifice comes to us as a Law from a Superior Being. Heathen nations have recognized the efficacy of sacrifice and offerings.

Man without Law was an impossibility. No living thing can exist without some Law. Thus we look back to the first records of created living things for some Law. Science sheds a great, broad, and even scaring, light on the Law prevailing over inanimate nature. The seas and the fields obey it. But for us to make a record of Law as it made its beginning, is a task too great, and it is indeed then we feel that "fools may rush in" where better souls have had to languish in doubt.

Let us take the Law in the Bible as we can read it, and how few care to read it! There was a man once who had read the whole of the first five books through *twice*. Thinking there might be something to gain from such abnormal study, we propounded a few questions on this very subject. The result was a senseless repetition of verses from Leviticus. And yet, to tell the honest truth, there is very little left us to do but to *quote*. There is a little assistance we can give, and most thankful we are to have it in our power to do so. Let us all the time remember that the Bible Law is the sole foundation of every Law, Human and Divine, as far as we can discover. If it can be proved that the Babylonian record with its 40,000 year old kings is to be relied on, then by all means let us accept it.

We start with the sacrifice as the "*companion*" of the Law. No one can feel hurt by this. It is no good to any of us to ask whether Abel's sacrifice was according to revealed Law or anterior to it. It is plain that sacrifice came to be the great medium of the Law between man and the great prevailing Law. With this allowed, all the rest is easier to grasp. The early Law among the first people seemed to have no force but in its connection with some higher Power. This Power has been now deputed to earthly sources.

The writers of the Psalms represent to us a perfect intercourse with the Deity. The question then arises, "On what grounds was this intercourse conducted?" The answer seems clearly to be on the conditions of the Laws of sacrifice. Now, by comparing the elaborate list of these contained in Smith's "Dictionary of the Bible" with a very careful one in "Notes on the Hebrew Psalms," by W. R. Burgess (1879), we can make out a clear and very useful *resumé*. Leaving out the great sin offerings for the *whole people* and for the priests, we have the following sin offerings :—

1. For any sin of ignorance. Lev. iv. A most elaborate ceremonial of sacrifice and blood sprinkling. We should like to know when the "plea of ignorance" was done away with altogether, as we believe it has no force at all in modern Law.

2. For refusal to bear witness on oath. Lev. v. This is of very great interest in the light of recent legislation as to affirmation. We have come across many people, it is needless to add grossly ignorant, who have entirely lost sight of the obvious emphasis on the word "False" in the 9th Commandment, placing the whole force on the fact of "Witness."

3. The Laws as to defilement. These, we presume, have left no trace on modern Law.

4. The breach of a rash oath, the keeping of which would involve sin. Lev. v., 4. This opens a most interesting subject, but we have not space to enter upon it. From the days of Jephthah and his oath with regard to his daughter until this day, the question has been full of difficulties, and is divided amongst, perhaps, equal advocates for the two opposed views of it.

5. Sacrilege in ignorance, fraud, *suppressio veri*, and perjury, were punished by enforced compensation, and the addition of a fifth part of the value concerned in the matter to the priest, or to the person wronged.

6. Illtreatment of betrothed slaves. Lev. xix., 20. This is only curious, but at the same time

has a connection with late enactments in criminal Law.

7. The Law as to the powers of a father is extraordinary. When one considers the relation now existing and defined by our Law, the revolution is beyond all measure out of reasonable proportion. For a curse, a blow, or even wilful disobedience, the penalty was *death!*

8. The Law of usury is difficult, but the chief points are well known. The main principle of the Law prevails to this day. Let us only notice the striking fact that usury could not be exacted upon the Jews themselves. Does this not offer a fine comment on the grievous usury so cruelly enforced in after years by these people upon the *Gentile* races?

9. Debt. All debts were released at the seventh year. So there was a year of limitation.

10. Tithe. This Law has been so frequently and ably set forth, that it is entirely one's own fault if it needs any comment.

11. Poor Laws. These are conspicuous by their absence. There was a legal right of gleanings, a second tithe to be given in charity, and wages were to be paid day by day. (Deut. xxiv.)

A few rather important forms of legislation

must be placed here as addenda. We notice the entirely despotic power of the husband over the wife, and all belonging to her. Compare *our* useful but very late enactment as to married women's property, apart from her almost complete irresponsibility.

The slander against a wife's virginity is punished by a fine only, but the fact of its truth, and therefore no longer a slander, is punished by the death of the woman. This is a most striking proof of the lower room in social judgment awarded to the female Israelite. We notice also that the power of the master over his servant was absolute, but that the master suffered a penalty if his servant or slave died under castigation! Ex. xxi. If he was maimed, he was by this fact allowed his freedom. The rule as to *Hebrew* slaves is very interesting. It is too long to be quoted here, but it can be easily mastered by a reference to Ex. xxi., Deut. xv., Lev. xxv.

We notice that there is no protection *legally* allowed to *strangers*, and so we find kindness and protection enjoined as a sacred duty.

We believe that the old list of " Prohibited Degrees," which we saw placed in churches in our infancy, and is still to be seen, is in all respects enforced by our present Law. But we are not quite sure of this. We can only remember the vague sense of mystery underlying the clause, which was always put in the largest type :—

"A MAN MAY NOT MARRY HIS GRANDMOTHER."

Another most interesting Law must be carefully noticed, and if possible, more deeply studied. In cases of accidental homicide, there was mostly an "avenger of blood" to be looked for. To escape this untoward follower, cities of refuge or sanctuaries were named, and in these the poor wretch was safe until the death of the high priest.

As to the legal penalty of adultery, are we quite sure that, according to results, we have greatly improved upon the old Bible Law? Under this the punishment was *death* of *both offenders*. Was it the fear lest the population of the world should be so very seriously lessened that gradually brought this Law to less than a penal one, so that at this day a Royal "Commission" is placed on the offence in the shape of the absolute freedom of the offenders to seek for *another opportunity ?*

Just a few words more as to those who interpreted the Law. These were the Priests and the Levites. The "Judges," as we read of them in the book of that name, had, with the exception of Samuel, mostly to do with the settlement of political disputes, and the leading out of the people to victory or defeat, as the case might be. But in later times the power of the Sanhedrim was undoubtedly great.

The king's power was legally limited. But so it is, and has been, in all ages and in all dominions *in theory!* Yet we find Rehoboam expelled by Jereboam, and the latter as despotic as the former, just as we find a firm will in Cromwell after the despotism of Charles, in what had been then for centuries the most "Constitutionally" governed country in the world!

Sanctuaries.

By William E. A. Axon, f.r.s.l.

IN all ages men have attributed a special sanctity to certain localities, usually those devoted to the purposes of worship, and this sentiment has in many lands been utilised in the interests of mercy by exempting those within the precincts from arrest for some, or even all, crimes and offences. In the earlier stages of development, the punishment of crime was not regarded as a duty of the community, but as an obligation, or privilege of the injured or of those nearest to him in blood or social relationship. Thus the son of a murdered man had the right to murder the murderer. The general principle of the earlier forms of justice is the *lex talionis*, but the infliction of the penalty was mostly in the discretion of the avenger. He might be afraid to attempt to slay a strong or powerful homicide, and be willing to pardon the offence for a money consideration. A criminal who took refuge in a sacred place secured at least a breathing time in which his friends might effect a compromise with his adversary. Greece had its famous *asyla*, but the custom of our own country was probably influenced from Hebrew rather than classical sources. In the narrative of the death of Joab, the hesitation of Benaiah shows that it was unusual to slay one who had taken hold of the horns of the altar. The six Cities of Refuge were appointed as places of safety for involuntary homicides, where they were protected from the avenger of blood. Amongst our Anglo-Saxon ancestors, the Church exerted a moderating influence. Every consecrated church had the right to shelter the fugitive from justice for seven days, and when the building was needed, he might be placed in a house provided for that purpose by the church, which was not to have more doors than the church itself. If the criminal was dragged forth from his refuge, the violaters of the sanctuary were fined in varying degrees according to the rank of the ecclesiastical edifice. In addition to the inherent right of each church, special privileges were conferred on certain places by the exercise of the royal prerogative. In 1378, it was decided that the property of fraudulent debtors who had taken sanctuary

SANCTUARIES.

should be liable for the satisfaction of the claims of their creditors. In 1486, Pope Innocent VIII. issued a bull relating to English sanctuaries, by which it was provided that when the refugee left his asylum, he lost his right of protection, even though he subsequently returned to the sanctuary. At the same time, the king was empowered to appoint keepers to look after those who having been accused of treason, had taken sanctuary.

Great changes were made in the law during the reign of Henry VIII. Traitors were wholly exempted from the privilege; those abjuring the realm were not actually banished, but were to remain throughout life in the sanctuary, and if they left it and committed any offence, they might then be brought to trial. All inmates were to wear a badge twenty inches in length and breadth, were forbidden the use of weapons, and were not to leave their lodgings between sunrise and sunset. In 1538, the right of sanctuary was further restricted, and Wells, Manchester, Northampton, York, Derby, and Launceston were declared sanctuaries. Manchester found this privilege to be of such doubtful value that two years later it was transferred to Chester, and afterwards to Stafford. In the reign of James I., the right of sanctuary was abolished almost everywhere. The Palatine Counties had their special sanctuaries. In Cheshire, Hoole Heath, Overmarsh, and Rudheath were such places of refuge. The abbey of Vale Royal had also a grant. But generally the County Palatine of Chester was a place of resort for those who had come into conflict with the law in other parts of the kingdom, and it was not until the reign of Charles II. that the king's writ ran in the palatinates and other privileged places. Many privileged places in London, Westminster, and Southwark were brought within the regular jurisdiction in the reign of William III. and George II.

We have an instructive picture of the working of the sanctuary system in the case of Manchester. The Act of 32 Hen. VIII., c. 8, abolished the right of refuge in all places except, and the exception is a considerable one—churches, hospitals, and churchyards. Perhaps a more important exception was that sanctuary was to be denied to those guilty of murder, rape, highway robbery, burglary, house-burning, or sacrilege. Whilst abolishing many sanctuaries, certain additional places were named as cities of refuge for minor offenders. One of these was Manchester. A year later the town petitioned to be relieved from this distinction. The inhabitants set forth that Manchester had a great trade in the bleaching of linen yarn, and in the making of linen and woollen cloths and dressing of cotton, and that the influx of dissolute persons to the sanctuary had caused serious damage to the prospects of the town, which, having no mayor, sheriff, or bailiff, and no jail, was badly circumstanced for dealing with these lawless invaders. The request was granted, and the sanctuary removed from Manchester to Chester. But the city of the Deva found it desirable to obtain relief, and a further removal was made to Stafford.

The fridstool at Hexham still remains, although nearly everything else of the Saxon foundation has perished. This "chair of peace" was the central point of the sanctuary, which extended a mile around. A Durham example of the working of the law may be cited.

"Memorandum : That on the 13th day of the month of May, A.D. 1464, one Colson, of Wolsyngham, Durham, who had been detected in a theft, and therefore put and detained in gaol, at length contrived to escape, and fled to the Cathedral Church of Durham, in order to avail himself of its immunities, and whilst he was there standing near the bier of St. Cuthbert, prayed, that a Coroner might be assigned to him. Upon John Raket, Coroner of the Ward of Chester in Strata (sic) coming to him, the same Colson confessed the felony, making upon the spot the corporeal oath that he abjured the realm of England, and would withdraw from it as soon as he could conveniently, and would never return thither, and which oath he took at the bier of St. Cuthbert in the presence of Master George Cornworth, Sacristan of the Cathedral Church of Durham; Ralph Bows, Knight and Sheriff of Durham; John Raket (the Coroner); Robert Thrylkett, Deputy Sheriff; Hugh Holand, and Nicholas Dixson, and of many others; by reason of which renunciation and oath all the dress of the said Colson belonged to the said Sacristan and his office; wherefore the said Colston was enjoined to take off to his shirt all his garments, and deliver them to the aforesaid Sacristan, and he did so, placing them all into his possession, the Sacristan gave up and delivered to him again, gratuitously, all his dress that he had up to this occasion been clothed in; and after that Colstone withdrew from the Church, and was handed over to the nearest constable by the aforesaid sheriff, and so on from constables to constables, holding a white cross made of wood as a fugitive, and so he was to be conducted to the nearest seaport to take vessel as one never to return. This was done on the day, month, and year aforesaid." *

---

* This and other documents have been collected by Mr. T. J. de' Massinghi, whose monograph on "Sanctuaries" (Stafford, 1888) is the chief source of information on the subject.

SANCTUARIES.

The system was one that led to gross abuse. It was held that the right did not extend to others than those whose offences entailed forfeiture of life and limb, but in practice knavish debtors, fraudulent executors, etc., availed themselves of the protection. There was plenty of scope for dispute as to jurisdiction. In 1427, the Abbot of Beaulieu was required to give proof of his right to shelter William Wawe, who is described as as heretic, traitor, common highwayman and public robber. "Wille Wawe was hanged," is the sum of the matter as recorded by Stowe. Between 1478 and 1539, at Durham, 283 persons took refuge who were, as principals or accessories, accused of homicide. There were sixteen debtors, four horse-stealers, nine cattle-stealers, and four house-breakers. One had been charged with rape, and seven with theft. One had been backward in his accounts, one had harboured a thief, and one had failed to prosecute. Sir John Holland, in revenge for the death of his esquire, killed the son and heir of Hugh, second Earl of Stafford, and then took sanctuary at Beverley. The murderer, in this case, was the half-brother of Richard II., but it was with great difficulty that the king was induced to grant a pardon.

The church of St. John of Beverley had a charter from Athelstan, and near the altar was the Fridstool, or chair of peace, "to which what criminal soever flies hath full protection." The privilege extended for a radius of about a mile round the minster, and the limits were marked by stone crosses. Infraction of the right of sanctuary was punishable by severe penalties, and to take a refugee from the Fridstool was to incur both secular and ecclesiastical penalties, the latter extending to excommunication.*

The widow of Edward IV. fled with her younger children for safety to the sanctuary of Westminster after her eldest son had fallen into the keeping of the Duke of Gloucester. Sir Thomas More reports the discussion in the Council of the Protector, and the arguments used by Cardinal Bourchier, which induced the queen to give up the Duke of York. The boy king, who was never crowned, and his brother were murdered in the Tower. It is noteworthy that this unfortunate monarch was born in the sanctuary of Westminster when his father was in exile. Skelton, the poet, died in this same sanctuary.

* See Andrews' "Old Church Lore," 1891, and the authorities there cited.

The privileges of the sanctuary were not always respected. When Geoffrey, Archbishop of York, took refuge in St. Martin's Priory, Dover, he was dragged from the altar in his pontifical robes by order of the bishop of Ely, who was then Chancellor of the Kingdom. But this arbitrary proceeding was not the least of the causes of the downfall of William of Longchamp. When William Longbeard, who had been condemned to death, took sanctuary at St. Mary-le-Bow, Hubert de Burgh ordered the church tower to be set on fire to compel him to come forth. Longbeard abandoned his place of refuge, and was dragged to Tyburn, and there hanged. But although de Burgh was Archbishop of Canterbury and Justiciary of the Kingdom, and the Church was his own peculiar, his violation of sanctuary led to the loss of his great secular dignity. Later, when he had himself to seek refuge, a great debate arose as to his having been forcibly taken from a sanctuary, and he was restored to its protection, and escaped to Wales.

Whilst the same rights of sanctuary existed in Ireland and in Wales, they were apparently not made use of to any great extent. In Scotland, the churches of Wedale, near Galashiels, and of

Lesmahagow, near Lanark, were the most famous of the religious sanctuaries. The latter had also a royal charter from David I. These sanctuaries ended with the Reformation. The abbey of Holyrood and its precincts, which include Arthur's Seat and the Queen's Park, gave protection to debtors until, by the abolition of imprisonment for debt, its privileges ceased to have any meaning. One of those who thus sought refuge at Holyrood during a part of his career was Thomas de Quincey.

Sanctuaries probably served a useful purpose in ages when the law was harsh and indiscriminate in its punishment of offenders. The limited protection afforded by the Church sanctuaries at least gave an opportunity for the first heat of revengeful feeling to subside, and the greater sanctuaries protected not merely vulgar offenders, but those whom the stormy tide of politics had placed at the mercy of their enemies. As the law became stronger, and the course of justice more certain, the need for these refuges ended, and those that continued were public nuisances, and mere centres of crime and anarchy, such as Scott has described for us in his picture of Alsatia. We may be thankful that sanctuaries are now merely objects of antiquarian interest and speculation.

Trials in Superstitious Ages.

By Ernest H. Rann.

IN superstitious ages, when belief in the power of the law to adjust all quarrels, to hold the balance equally between man and man, and to accord to each one his rights, was less prevalent than it is at the present day, disputants naturally resorted to other tribunals for the settlement of their claims. A perfect system of law was impossible; what law existed was arbitrarily administered, often for the benefit of the most powerful litigant, and the claimant with only justice on his side often had the mortification of seeing a verdict given against him. During the development of a system of law-giving, when the accumulated experience of humanity had not sufficed to produce perfection, man in his darkness, his ignorance, and superstition, turned to the supernatural, and devised certain ceremonies by which the judgment of God might be evoked to demonstrate the guilt or innocence of the accused.

The antiquity of the ordeal, as it was called, cannot be measured. Such a form of trial is found to have existed in the earliest ages, and even now traces of it linger among savage tribes of the earth. In Africa especially the ordeal is well known. During his travels among the negro tribes north of the Zambesi, Dr. Livingstone encountered the curious practice of the "mauvi," which consisted of making all the women of a tribe drink an infusion of "goho," for the purpose of ascertaining which of them had bewitched a particular man. The accused women were drawn up in a row before the hut of the king, and the draught administered to them. Those who were unable to retain the horrible decoction, and vomited, were considered innocent of the charge: those who were purged were adjudged guilty, and put to death by burning.

The Calabar bean is also used by the natives of Africa in the form of an emulsion as an ordeal for persons accused of witchcraft, proof of innocence consisting of ability to throw off the poison by vomiting. Among the Barotse tribes the process is conducted by deputy, the testing liquid being poured down the throat of a dog or cat, and the accused person being treated according to the effect produced on the animal. Among the Dyak tribes lumps of salt are thrown into a bowl of water by the accuser and accused, and judgment is given against the owner whose lump disappears first. Another method adopted by the Dyaks is for each of the two parties to choose a mollusc, and to squeeze over it a few drops of lime-juice; the owner of the mollusc which moves first under the acid stimulant losing the case. Ratzel mentions that among the Malay tribes ordeals by fire, ducking, pulling a ring out of boiling water, or licking red-hot iron, are still frequent. Where the ordeal fails to produce the desired result, wager of battel, in reality another form of ordeal, is resorted to. Among the Tagals it is usual to light a consecrated candle, and to consider the person guilty of the crime under consideration to whom the candle flame is blown during the performance of the ceremony. The Igorrotes have a more painful method of fixing guilt. The accuser and the accused are placed together; the backs of their heads are scratched with a sharply-pointed bamboo stick, and the man who loses most blood also loses his case.

In Hawaii ordeals are administered by the priests, the suspected person being compelled to hold his hands over consecrated water, and adjudged guilty if the liquid trembles in the vessel while the priest looks at him. The Siamese have a form of ordeal which consists of making the two parties to a suit swallow consecrated purgative pills, the man who retains them for the greater length of time winning the case.

Even among the comparatively enlightened races of the peninsula of India, ordeals of the most elaborate and curious character are practised at the present time. Warren Hastings mentions that in his day no fewer than nine forms were in use among the Hindoos. The ordeal of the balance was commonly employed, and is still in force in certain districts. The beam is adjusted, and both scales made perfectly even. After the accused has been bathed in sacred water, and the deities worshipped, he is placed in the scale-pan and carefully weighed. When he is taken out the Pandits pronounce an incantation, and place round his head a piece of paper setting forth the charge against him. Six minutes later he again enters the scale, and the balance is called upon to show his fault or innocence. If he weigh more than before, he is held guilty; if less, innocent;

TRIALS IN SUPERSTITIOUS AGES.   27

if exactly the same, he must be weighed a third time, when, according to the *Mitácsherá*, a difference in his weight will be observable. Should the balance break down, the mishap would be considered as proof of the man's guilt.

The ordeal of the balance is not altogether unknown in English history, for an incident is recorded in which Susannah Haynokes, of Aylesbury, was accused of bewitching her neighbour's spinning-wheel, and preventing it from working properly. Susannah loudly protested her innocence, and demanded an ordeal to prove it. She was taken to the church, and weighed in a semi-nude condition against a copy of the Bible, and being able to outweigh the Scriptures, was considered to be innocent of the offence charged against her. Possibly it never occurred to the owner of the spinning-wheel that lack of oil was the cause of its refusal to go round.

Among other ordeals in use by the Hindoos is that of iron, the accused being required to lick a red-hot bar of the metal. If his tongue be burnt, he is considered guilty, if not, he is reckoned innocent, but it cannot be supposed that among tribes addicted to this practice the injury to the tongue is considered sufficient punishment for the offence with which the suspect is charged. The poison ordeal, employed also, it may be noted, by the Hovas of Madagascar, is commonly practised. A small quantity of *vishanága*, a poisonous root, is mixed with clarified butter, which the accused must eat from the hand of a Brahman. If the poison produce no visible effect, he is absolved; otherwise, condemned. In other cases the hooded snake called *nága* is placed in a deep earthen pot, from which the accused has to take a ring, seal, or coin without being bitten, when he is considered innocent. In trial by the Cósha the accused is made to drink three draughts of water in which images of the Sun, of Déví, and other deities have been washed. If, within fourteen days, he is afflicted with any form of sickness, he is considered guilty.

For the fire ordeal an excavation is made in the ground, and filled with burning pippal wood. Into this a person must walk bare-footed without hurt in order to prove his innocence. Hot oil ordeals are also in force, when the accused has to thrust his hand into the liquid without being burned; and chewing a grain of consecrated rice, which, if it comes from the man's mouth dry or stained with blood, is considered proof of his guilt. At other times a silver image of the Genius of Justice, called *Dharma*, is thrown with an image of iron or clay, called *Adharma*, into an earthen jar; and the accused is acquitted if he bring out the silver image, but condemned if he draw forth the iron.

The history of the middle ages furnishes numerous examples of ordeals employed in the settlement of disputes, which in the absence of a strong and impartial system of law-giving, found great favour with the people of all ranks. They were peculiarly distinguished by the appellation of *Judicium Dei*, or judgments of God, and sometimes called *vulgaris purgatio*. The law of the Church sanctioned the ordeal throughout Europe for a considerable period, and faculties were freely given by the clergy for the performance of these strange ceremonials. Indeed, the whole business, as a judgment of God, was frequently conducted by the servants of the Church, always in consecrated ground, and the sacred edifice itself was occasionally requisitioned in order to add greater solemnity to the proceedings. The ordeal of fire, practised, curiously enough, by the Greeks in the time of Sophocles, was allowed only to persons of high rank. The accused was required to carry a piece of red-hot iron for some distance in his hand, or to walk nine feet, bare-footed and blindfold, over red-hot ploughshares. The hands or feet were then immediately bound up, and inspected three days afterwards. If, on examination, no injury was visible, the accused was considered innocent; if traces of the burning remained, he was reckoned guilty, and received punishment commensurate with his offence, without any discount for the harm he had already suffered.

The most notable historic instance of this form of ordeal is that of Queen Emma, mother of Edward the Confessor. She was accused of a criminal intrigue with Alwyn, Bishop of Winchester, and condemned to the ordeal of fire, which, on this particular occasion, took the form of nine red-hot ploughshares, laid lengthwise at irregular intervals, over which she was required to walk with bandaged eyes. She passed successfully through the severe trial, and at the conclusion innocently asked when the ordeal was about to begin. The Queen's innocence was, to the popular mind, established more substantially than would have been possible in any existing court of law. She was not the only gainer by the restoration of her reputation, for in consideration of the success which had attended her, she settled twenty-one manors on the Bishopric and Church of Winchester.

In the Eastern Empire the fire ordeal was largely used by the Emperor Theodore Lascoris for the discovery of the origin of the sickness with which he was afflicted. His majesty attributed the malady to magic, and all suspected persons were required to handle red-hot iron in order to establish their guilt or innocence, "thus joining," as an ancient scribe exclaims, "to the most dubious crime in the world the most dubious proof of innocence."

Fire, as we have said, was employed for persons of high rank: those of baser degree, especially bondsmen and rustics, were tried by the ordeal of boiling water. "I will go through fire and water for my friend" was a common expression in the middle ages, and, though having lost its original significance, the saying has persisted to the present time as a declaration of self-sacrifice. The accused person was required to take a stone from a pan of boiling water, to insert the hand and wrist into the liquid, and in case of the triple ordeal, to plunge the arm in up to the elbow. When cold water was employed, and in cases of witchcraft this was generally resorted to, the suspect was flung into a river or pond. If he floated without appearance of swimming, he was pronounced innocent; if he sank, he was condemned as guilty —rather a superfluous proceeding, considering that the man was in all probability already drowned.

It would be going too far to assert that in all cases these ordeals were carried out with the strictest impartiality and consideration for the ends of justice. Means were not unknown to circumvent the peculiar forms of the trial, and precautions were often taken by the clergy, as might have been done in the case of Queen Emma, to protect those whom they desired to clear of suspicion. It is a well-known fact that white-hot iron may be licked with impunity, and the Mevleheh dervishes are proficient in the trick of holding red-hot iron between their teeth. Sometimes cold iron, painted red, was employed, and at others the fire reduced in temperature at the critical moment, the suspect receiving only such injury as would heal in the three days allowed before his hand was examined. Artificial preparations were frequently employed, while the suspect had at times the option of going alone into the church, and in all cases of keeping the crowd of spectators at a distance, which made minute inspection of the proceedings impossible.

Another form of ordeal was the *judicium crucis*, or trial of the Cross, employed largely in criminal cases. When an accused person had declared his innocence on oath, and appealed to the judgment of the Cross, two sticks were prepared precisely like one another. The figure of the Cross was cut upon one of these sticks, and the other left blank. Each of them was wrapped in fine white wool, and laid upon the altar or the relics of the saints, after which a prayer was uttered that God might discover by unmistakable signs whether the prisoner was innocent or guilty. The priest then approached the altar, took up one of the sticks, and uncovered it. If it happened to be the stick marked with the cross, the prisoner was pronounced innocent; if it were the other, he was condemned as guilty. A different form of this ordeal was adopted when the judgment of the Cross was invoked in civil cases. The judges and all parties to the suit assembled in the church. Representatives, generally the youngest and strongest priests, were then chosen, and required to stand one on each side of a crucifix. At a given signal they stretched out their arms at full length, so as to form a cross with their body, and in this painful posture they continued to stand during divine service. The party whose representative dropped his arms first, or shifted his position, lost his cause. History records a dispute over a monastery, between the Bishop of Paris and the Abbot of St. Denis, which was settled in this manner. A crowd assembled, and arranged bets on the result, but those who supported the Bishop's man were sadly disappointed, for he dropped his arms at an early stage, and lost the cause of his employer. The ordeal of the Cross was abolished by Louis de Debonnaire in 816, on the ground that it was irreverent in character.

Ecclesiasticism also played a prominent part in the ordeal of the corsnedd, to which persons accused of robbery had to submit. The corsnedd was a piece of bread made of unleavened barley, to which cheese made of ewe's milk in the month of May was added. Over the whole, one ounce in weight, a form of exorcism was uttered, desiring of the Almighty that the corsnedd might cause convulsions and paleness, and find no passage, if the man were really guilty, but might turn to health and nourishment if he were innocent. The practice is strongly remindful of the trial of jealousy in use among the Israelites, by which an unfaithful woman was compelled to drink holy water containing dust of the floor of the tabernacle, the belief being that she would be stricken with illness if she were guilty. The corsnedd was given to the suspected person, who at the same time read the sacrament. Godwin, Earl of Kent, was, in the reign of Edward the Confessor, accused of murder, and forced to the ordeal of the corsnedd, when, according to ancient chroniclers, the consecrated food stuck in his throat, and caused his death. Both the expressions, "I will take the sacrament upon it," and "May this morsel be my last," are supposed to have been derived from this curious form of lawgiving. A somewhat similar custom is in vogue in Russia at the present day. Balls of bread are made and dropped into consecrated water, the priest meanwhile reciting the formula :—"Ivan Ivanoff, if you are guilty, as this ball falls to the bottom, so your soul will fall into hell." As a rule the culprit confesses immediately. In Ceylon, also, a similar form of ordeal is by no means unusual. A man suspected of theft is required to bring the person he holds in greatest affection before the judge, and placing a heavy stone on the head of his substitute, say, "May this stone crush thee to death if I am guilty of the offence." The Tartar sets a wild bear and a hatchet before the tribunal, saying as he does so, "May the bear devour me, and the hatchet chop off my head, if I am guilty of the crime laid to my charge."

Another form of ordeal which was cherished and practised with assiduity was that of the bier, founded on the belief that the body of a murdered man would show signs, by bleeding or movement, when his assassin approached. The accused had to place his hand on the naked breast of the corpse, and declare his innocence, though the slightest change in the body was considered proof of his guiltiness. This method of finding out murderers had its origin, it is believed, in Denmark, where it was in the first instance adopted by King Christian II. for the discovery of the murderer of one of his courtly followers. The belief has survived to a certain extent to the present day, for even English peasants still expect all persons present at a funeral to touch the body in proof of their bearing no ill-will towards the dead man.

TRIALS IN SUPERSTITIOUS AGES.

Not so frequently employed, but still occasionally met with in ancient history, was the ordeal of compurgation, where the innocence of the accused was sworn to by his friends, and judgment went against the party whose kindred refused to come forward, or who failed to provide the necessary number of compurgators. It was a conflict of numerical strength, and the higher number carried the day.

Another custom, still surviving, was to tie a key in a Bible opened at Psalm L, verse 18, "When thou sawest a thief, then thou consentedst with him," and balance the whole, the belief being that the book would turn in the hands of a guilty person.

Challenging the accuser to mortal combat was a proceeding which found much favour with the warlike spirit of the middle ages. Of course it was considered that Providence would defend the right, even if a miracle were needful, but nevertheless each party placed considerable reliance on his own strength of arm and fighting skill. These judicial combats were in ancient times practised among the Jews, and were also common in Germany in remote ages, though they do not find mention in Anglo-Saxon laws, and were apparently not in use in England until after the Norman Conquest. In Germany a bier was placed in the midst of the lists, accuser and accused stood respectively at the head and foot, and remained for some minutes in profound silence before they commenced fighting. Civil, criminal, and military cases were, in the absence of sufficient direct evidence, decided by means of the judicial combat or wager of battel. The offended party had the right to challenge his accuser to settle the dispute by force of arms, and the forms and ceremonies connected with the trial are well illustrated in the opening scenes of "King Richard II." The combat took place in the presence of the court itself, Heaven being expected to give the victory to the innocent or injured party. It was commonly resorted to in charges of treason, as in the above-mentioned dispute between Henry Bolingbroke and Thomas Mowbray, when the ceremonies were of an imposing character. As in the majority of ordeals, deputies could be chosen to perform the requisite duties, but the principals were in all cases answerable for the consequences. No commoner was allowed to challenge a peer of the realm, nor could the citizens of London, for some obscure reason, indulge in these popular forms of legal administration. Each of the combatants professed his willingness to make good his claims, body for body—

"For what I speak
My body shall make good upon this earth,
Or my divine soul answer it in heaven."

Neither sorcery nor witchcraft had to be employed, and the battel was to continue until the shades of evening had fallen, and the stars appeared. If the accused were killed, his blood was attainted, but if he were only vanquished, he was immediately condemned to an ignominious death by hanging, providing he accepted his fate without demur. The defeated party, however, might crave his life, in which case he was allowed to live as a recreant, on condition that he retracted unreservedly the false statements that he had sworn.

At the Durham Assizes, on August 6, 1638, a wager of battel was offered and accepted, for deciding the rights to land at Thickley, between Ralph Claxton, demandant, and Richard Lilburne, tenant. According to an old chronicle, "the defendant appeared at 10 o'clock in the forenoon, by his attorney, and brought in his champion,

George Cheney, in full array, with his stave and sandbag, who threw down his gauntlet on the floor of the court, with five small pieces of coin in it. The tenant then introduced his champion, William Peverell, armed in the same manner, who also threw down his gage." But the champions, instead of being allowed to fight, were ordered to appear at the Court of Pleas in the following month. Legal arguments followed, and the trial by battel was eventually postponed indefinitely.

In criminal trials no deputies were allowed, and the parties were compelled to settle their quarrel in person, unless one of them was a woman, an infant, or a man over the age of sixty, or was afflicted with lameness or blindness. In the case of any of these disqualifications, trial by jury could be claimed and insisted upon. One of the most remarkable wagers of battel occurred in 1817. A young woman named Mary Ashford, living at Erdington, near Birmingham, was supposed to have been murdered early one morning when returning from a dance. Suspicion fell on Abraham Thornton, a partner of the previous night, who was tried for the crime and acquitted. Evidence for another trial was collected, and Thornton was *appealed* by William Ashford, the direct heir male of the murdered woman. But when the proceedings commenced, Thornton's counsel took refuge under a very old Act, by which no man could be tried on a second charge of murder, on which he had been acquitted, except by wager of battel before the king, between the heir-at-law of the person murdered and the accused. The appellant, Mary Ashford's brother, declined the combat on the ground of physical inferiority, and Thornton was discharged. Immediately afterwards the antiquated law was removed from the Statute Book.

This marked the end of trials by ordeal as recognised by law. The process of extermination had long been in progress, but popular opinion was against reform, and certain of these curious customs survived. Athough the clergy had at first taken part in these ceremonials, and presided over them in church, they came in time to discountenance them. The canon law declared against ordeals as being the work of the Devil, and a decree to this effect was issued in the eighteenth canon of the fourth Lateran Council in November, 1215. Upon this authority it was thought proper, says Blackstone (as had been done in Denmark a century ago), "to disuse and abolish these trials entirely in our courts of justice by an Act of Parliament, Henry III., according to Sir Edward Coke, or rather by an order of the King in Council." The actual date of the abolition of ordeals by fire and water was 1261 On the Continent these forms of trial had been abolished by civil and ecclesiastical law much earlier, although in 1498 an attempt was made to test the doctrine of Savonarola by means of a challenge from one of his disciples to a Franciscan friar to walk through a pile of burning wood. Old customs die hard, and the incident is a curious and interesting instance of the persistence of a popular form of trial even among the members of a party by which it had been condemned.

On Symbols.

By George Neilson.

THE wayward fancies of mankind are well illustrated in the diversity of symbolic observances, some never losing their meaning, some absolutely unintelligible in their historic form, and some as much characterised by a befitting dignity, as others are by the want of it. All once were self-explanatory and possessed a measure of propriety proportioned to the state of the people amidst whom they originated. But tradition is long, centuries elapse, each modifying a ceremony, and when the procedure emerges within the knowledge of record, it has often so lost touch with its surroundings, that it is hopeless to speculate how it arose.

Symbols are drawn from and applied to every field of human activity. Of course in a general sense man expresses himself only so, and a regular alphabet is but a comparatively trifling advance on the language of signs. What we call civilization, is at bottom little more than a clear recognition of certain symbols of government. The Queen's crown, the Judge's ermine, the Mayor's mace, what are they else? The sceptre is only a glorified stick, of which the policeman's baton is a humbler shape. Each embodies the great thought that behind it stands a nation's determination to be ruled by law.

In the history of law, symbol and the traces of symbol meet us at every turn. The middle ages teemed with them. Roman law had bequeathed not a few. Perhaps the most wondrous of them all is one that has long ceased to have any legal connection, although its mark is all-powerful over civilisation. How daring was the imagination which prompted the choice, for the heraldic badge of christianity, of the dread emblem of capital punishment by crucifixion! In the pure domain of the law of the early and middle ages, a perfect wilderness of symbols presents itself to eyes which strive to explore the origins of institutions.

Law is ever beset by a tendency towards formalism, and in early times a severe insistence upon ceremony, no doubt, gave prominence and prescriptive sanction to symbolic acts. Law and custom after all only mean that the way things were done yesterday is the safest way of doing them to-day. The acceptance of a common form implies a very large public consent, which is equally necessary to its abrogation, once it is accepted. No small part of its value lies in its certainty, "certainty which," Coke well says, "is the mother of quiet and repose."

Hence the fixity and longevity of many emblematic methods of performing acts affecting status or property rights. The constitution or discharge of slavery, or the transfer of a slave from one master to another, had a variety of set forms. A freeman might deliver himself to serfage by putting a leathern thong upon his neck. When a church was the donee, the ceremony might take place at the altar, and the man present himself there with cords round his throat. "Thus he offered himself," says an old record, "to the Almighty Lord." A coin or two on the head was also a customary part of the process. In the manumission or liberation of the slave, these coins struck off the head served the purpose of declaring him free, as did the companion symbol of open doors, or the placing him at four cross roads, and bidding him go whither he would. Another common symbol of enfranchisement was the delivery of an arrow, thought to denote the right confined to freemen of bearing arms.

Even a short account of legal symbols would make a very large treatise. Single instances such as the ring, the staff, the glove, and the horn would each furnish material for an elaborate monograph. The theme would call for a discussion of the great war of investitures, and would touch very many points of ecclesiastical, civil, and criminal law and history. The scope of the present unambitious article is only directed to a few illustrations in relation to the transfer of land, the act of divesting the old proprietor and clothing the new with his rights. Although such symbols usually had a connexion with the subject conveyed, there are many types in which that connexion is not readily traceable. Why for example amongst the Saxons should a resignation of all interest in an estate have been made by a gesture with curved fingers? One can understand why a sod should be so often a token, but why does the glove play so large a part in Merovingian and Carolingian conveyancing? Was it, indeed, as German scholars speculate, because the donor metaphorically took it off and the donee put it on, making his the covered hand, the *vestita manus*, that would defend the land conveyed? How came an eleventh century magnate to attest his renunciation of justiciary rights to a monastery "by cutting off the top of the silk band by which his fur robes were fastened to his breast, and with that segment re-investing three monks therein?" In this case a portion of that silken band was carefully sewn up, as an adminicle of evidence, in the writ recording the transaction. How again came it that a claim of feudal service might be departed from by the delivery and placing of a wand *(virgula)* upon the altar? All these are much more personal symbols than real. They are mainly guarantees of the grantor's good faith. They do not seem to be primarily emblems of possession. The contrast between these two classes will be best appreciated by considering types of the latter.

When a purchaser proceeded to set up fresh boundary marks, or to take a spade and dig, or when he received delivery of a sod with grass or shrubbery upon it, or lifted from the ground the charter granted by the seller with amongst other things a sod laid thereon, the act of seisin, the formal occupation is visibly completed. Of this class of symbol, the sod *(cespes)* is probably the best and most typical for a few words of illustration. We read of litigants laying judicial claim to land in the mall or public court by putting their spears into a sod, representative of the subject in dispute. We hear of the sods being cut in the shape of bricks, and of their being preserved as memorials, with the twigs growing in and incorporated with them. We hear of sods offered on the altar when the grant of land was being made to a church. We hear of transfer from one vassal to another being accomplished by the grantor delivering the sod to the over-lord, and the latter passing it on to the grantee.

Of all the symbols employed in connection with feoffments, however, the rod *(festuca)* had the widest vogue on the continent. Not that it was restricted to transactions in land; it was a more or less lineal descendant of the Roman stipulation, a contract visibly expressed by the parties breaking a straw between them. Under Charlemagne a renunciation by certain priests was made by them "holding straws in their hands and casting them from them before God and his angels." Later this appears as a recognised method of renunciation, but with a rod substituted for the straw. In some cases the fact of renunciation is emphasised by the rod being not only thrown to the ground by the resigner, but trodden under foot when there. The rôle of the *festuca* was peculiarly important amongst the Frankish peoples.* Galbert of Bruges, a Flemish twelfth century historian, states that the counts of Flanders gave investitures to their vassals, after receiving their fealty and homage, by a wand *(virgula)* held in hand, and he has a dramatic passage describing how the people of Bruges, in token of their renunciation of their feudal bond to Hacket the castellan, "picking up bits of stick exfestucated their homage and fealty," *i.e.* cast the rods from them, and so doing severed all connexion with their former chief.

In England and in Scotland, this rod symbol *(fustis et baculus)* also played a large part. Bracton referred it specially to land without houses. Tenure by the verge, a species of copyhold, had its name, we learn from Littleton, from

* The material facts in this paper up to this point are derived from Thevenin's *Textes relatifs aux Institutions privées* and *Du Cange art. investitura.*

un petite verge, delivered by the old tenant to the steward or bailiff of the manor, who re-delivered it to the new holder. Jordan Fantosme tells us that when Brien, messenger of Ranulf Glanvil, in 1174, announced in Westminster the capture of the Scottish King at Alnwick, Henry II. rewarded him for his good news by handing him a stick *(bastuncel),* which vested him in ten librates of land. In Scotland the feudal resignation by a vassal to his overlord for the re-investure of a fresh owner was effected by "staff and baton" *(fustis et baculus),* and references to those symbols occurred in every day conveyancing until far into the present century. Indeed this picturesque ritual was, strictly speaking, not abrogated, although made unnecessary, by the Act 8 and 9 Victoria ch. 35.

The commonest conveyancing symbol for land in England was the formal delivery of turf or twig of the ground conveyed, made by a representative of the grantor, to a representative of the grantee. The most familiar in Scotland was the handing over of "earth and stone." This latter was the normal form of seisin, and its history goes far back, not only in Scotland, but on the continent as well. A curious Saxon legend attests this. Widukind narrates that some Saxons, having landed from their ships in Thuringia, one of them, wearing a golden torque and bracelets, met a Thuringian, who asked if he would sell his ornaments. The sly Saxon entered into an odd transaction; the Thuringian gave him in exchange for his gold, a lapful of soil. The Thuringians rejoiced exceedingly over the smart bargain their countryman had made, but changed their tune when soon afterwards the Saxons claimed the land as theirs, purchased with their own gold, and by force of arms made good the demand.

Our chronicles have a good many stories about symbols. In the Norman *Brevis Relatio*, a sketch of the origin of William the Conqueror, is told of his grandfather, Duke Richard the Good, that once when staying at a monastery, after prayer in the morning he laid a spindle on the altar. Upon being asked what it meant, he named the manor which he had by so homely a symbol bestowed for the good of his soul. When the infant William came into the world, it was said,—and afterwards noted as prophetic—that when they laid him down upon some straw, the little hands each clutched a handful. Acquisitive tendencies were foreshadowed! The *Roman de Rou* tells that in 1066, when William landed in England, he stumbled and fell, an omen which for the moment disconcerted his followers, but rising with a shout, he swore by the splendour of God that with his two hands he had taken possession of the land. Prompt to catch the occasion, one of his men ran forward to a cottage, tore a handful of thatch from the roof, and passed it to his chief, with the cry, "Receive this seisin,"— quasi-ceremonial words which with William's pious, "God be with me," the curious may compare with the formalities of English livery in deed, as described (sec. 59), in Coke upon Littleton.

The normal symbol of seisin for a house in England, was (before the Act 7 and 8 Victoria ch., 76, superseded these archaic ceremonies), was the ring or hasp of the door, known in Scotland for houses in burghs as "hasp and staple." In the latter country also, there were a good many special types of symbol characteristically appropriate to seisin in special kinds of property. Thus for mills "clap and hopper," for fishings "net and coble," for teinds (Anglice tithes) a sheaf of corn, for the patronage or

ON SYMBOLS. 53

advowson of a church a psalm-book and keys, attained the figurative purpose requisite. There were many others less familiar amongst them, one, a hat, worthy of a few words all to itself. Our own generation may not regard this as a particularly dignified symbol, but there is a cloud of witnesses to shew its very various applicability. The priest's cap or biretta was sometimes employed to instal him in a chaplainry or benefice. And apart from the place of the hat in the regulations of the tilting ring, it was occasionally used in Scotland as a symbol in connection with what were known as heirship goods. But it had in the twelfth century been accorded the very loftiest use to which secular symbolism could be turned. In 1175, King William the Lion, taken prisoner the year before, relinquished the independence of Scotland, and did homage to the English King at York, as a condition of his liberation. The contemporary records are silent regarding symbolic details, but in 1301 Edward I. stated in his letter to the Pope that "in token of his fealty, William the King of Scotland, had, on the altar of St. Peter's, at York, offered his cap *(chappelus)*, lance, and saddle, which until this day remain and are preserved in said church." Any incredulity which a fair-minded Scot can entertain, regarding this allegation that the freedom of his country was once symbolically surrendered in King William's cap, will be materially lessened, and Scottish patriotism so far consoled, by the recollection that under very similar circumstances the realm of England was in 1193 given away with the bonnet *(pilleus)* of the captive Richard I., who, thus (as Hoveden tells us), gave investiture of his kingdom to his arch-enemy, the Emperor Henry VI. This was, however, only formal: the Emperor at once re-invested King Richard in his realm with a double crown of gold, though subject to an annual tribute of £15,000—a business transaction painfully illustrative of the Christian chivalry of the Crusades.

The annals of Scotland boast one instance of a royal symbol much more regal than either of these two. About the beginning of the year 1124, King Alexander I., restoring by charter to the Bishopric of St. Andrews an extensive tract of land, completed the grant according to Andrew of Wyntoun (vii., 5), in a truly stately fashion. He—

ON SYMBOLS.

> Gert than to the awtare bryng
> Hys cumly sted off Araby
> Sadelyd and brydelyd costlykly
> Coveryd with a fayre mantlete
> Off precyous and fyne welvet
> Wyth his armwris off Turky
> That pryncys than oysid generaly
> And chesyd mast for thare delyte
> Wyth scheld and spere off sylvyr qwhyt.

It was a special occasion, for Bishop Robert's appointment, which had led to the grant, was a Scottish victory over the pretensions of the See of York. There is an appeal to the imagination so strong in the scene, that, in spite of the interval of 300 years betwixt the event and this oldest record of it, one is slow to offer any criticism on the charger; more especially as the entire verity of the silver spear is corroborated by Walter Bower's enshrining in his Scotichronicon the fact that in the fifteenth century it was doing duty as the shaft of the cross in the Cathedral. Yet the unexampled symbol, coupled with the analogy from York in 1175, compels the suggestion, that perhaps during these 300 years an original *capellus* may have been mis-read as *caballus*, or mistaken for Scottish *capul*, and thus by the magic of mistranslation, a king's cap *may* have been transmuted into an Arab steed.

Whilst of course a crown was the standard symbol of investiture for a kingdom, inferior rights of principality were often typified by other things, such as a sword, a spear, or a banner. And as feudal forms were observed in the bestowal, so were they sometimes in the taking away. England dispensed with several of her monarchs, but apparently in no case was a deposition attended by the feudal solemnities. In Scotland when, in 1296, King John Balliol was pulled out of the throne by the same hands as had placed him in it, Edward I. spared his vassal little of the indignity of the situation. Balliol, deprived of his royal ornaments, with the ermine stripped from his tabard, resigned his realm by the symbol of a white wand.

>Than this Jhon tuk a quhyt wand
>And gave wp in till Edwardis hand
>Off this Kynryk all the rycht.

No Scottish historian has noticed the absolute legal propriety of this, and it is worth noticing. By contemporary law *(Britton,* ii., 22), *une blaunche verge* was the recognised symbol of disseisin by consent. The thirteenth century was very particular, even in small things, about its law. *Disseisin*, provided for by statute of 1429, in disputed successions to real property, and known to Scotland as the breaking of seisin, was symbolically affected—*frangendo discum*—by the curiously expressive act of breaking a dish or dishes, with fire underneath.

Law under the Feudal System.

By Cuming Walters.

TO the historian proper feudalism presents a wide subject with diverse points of interest, but its legal aspect is comparatively a small matter, and it can be considered without detailed reference to the whole vast scheme which existed from early German and Gothic times, and overspread the greater part of Europe. It is a common error to suppose that it was introduced into England by the Normans. William the Conqueror only superimposed a French form of feudalism upon that which already existed; and all historians agree that the measures he adopted, the restrictions he made, and the original conditions he established, were evidence of his farseeing genius, and a masterpiece of statecraft. His was a feudalism which, while giving the lords great personal power and influence, retained them still as the servants of the king, and totally prevented them from using their strength against the throne. In this

LAW UNDER THE FEUDAL SYSTEM.

respect the feudal system in England never resembled that of Germany and France, or even that which the Norman barons established in Scotland. The Conqueror had no intention of allowing the owners of territory to supersede his own authority, and to be beyond the sovereign's control. While, therefore, he allowed them all liberty in dealing with their dependents, he made it impossible for them to defy his own authority, first by distributing their possessions so that they could not have a great army of followers at command, and, secondly, by insisting upon a formal declaration of allegiance from both the barons and their vassals. The former, therefore, were not beyond the law, and the latter had nominally, if not actually, some right of appeal to the monarch. These points it is necessary to bear in mind for a full understanding of legal procedure during the long period feudalism prevailed.

The feudal lord's claims upon his vassals were numerous. First came his claim to their military service. He could demand from them service as assessors in his courts of various fines and payments and confiscations of land. He could dispose of females in marriage ; not infrequently he consigned them to a debased existence. When the tenant was invested with possession of his feud or fief, he paid homage to his lord, that is, he proclaimed himself the "man" to help and to serve his master. Kneeling humbly before the baron, he took oath of fealty, and practically enslaved himself. It was here that King William showed his wisdom by ordaining that the oath of allegiance should be not only to the feudal superior, but to the monarch as the head of all, and thus he secured the ultimate service of all vassals to the crown, and deprived the barons of autocratic power.

The Saxon feudalism had been of the most tyrannical character, the owners of slaves making their own laws, and carrying them out with the utmost barbarism. Records exist which prove that for slight offences mistresses were accustomed to order their servants to be scourged to death, or subjected to fearful tortures. For breaking a dish, or spilling wine from a cup, for example, a servant might have his ears cut off, his nose slit, or suffer the loss of his hand, according to the caprice or fancy of his lord or lady. While murderers and robbers could find sanctuary in the Church, servants had no such refuge. They were torn away from the altar to which they clung in their terror, and none could or would intervene to protect them. According to the decree of King Ethelred, public punishments were to be mild, and death sentences were seldom to be passed; but the sovereign's wishes had no effect upon the treatment of bondmen. High-born women were as cruel as their husbands, and King Ethelred's own mother is said to have beaten him so severely when he was a child that he regarded whipping instruments with horror to the end of his life. Flagellation was not recognised as a legal punishment by the Saxons, though a husband might beat his wife and incur no penalty, while the whipping of slaves was accounted no more than the whipping of animals, and perhaps less. For all other classes money-fines were almost the only authorised penalty, a fixed price being set upon persons of different degrees. But the slave had no real value, and hence could be mutilated or killed at the pleasure of his lord.

The ideal of feudalism, never realised in England, was that the king and his tenants-in-chief should hold law-courts, which the tenant or the sub-tenants should be bound to attend to

have their cases tried according to statute rules.
But the system was only imperfectly carried out,
and the fact that the tenant-in-chief, or feudal
lord, had the right to levy taxes (called
"tallage" or "tailles") on his vassals, speedily
led to all sorts of tyranny and abuse. Still, the
feudal courts could not engross the legislation for
the excellent reason that the quick-witted Conqueror had preserved the Witanagenot and the
courts of the shire and the hundred to check the
barons. The latter made a big effort to introduce
the Continental system of feudalism, by which
each of them would have been supreme in his
domain; but the plans were defeated as we have
seen. William's successors were men of a
different stamp, and the system proved unworkable in the hands of weaker men. "The prince,"
says Hume, "finding that greater opposition was
often made to him when he enforced the laws
than when he violated them, was apt to render
his own will and pleasure the sole rule of government, and on every emergency to consider the
power of the persons whom he might offend
rather than the rights of those whom he might
injure." The mischievous course pleased none,
and the royal prerogative was at last system-

LAW UNDER THE FEUDAL SYSTEM. 63

atically assailed by the barons in the time of John, and the Magna Charta wrestled from him. The concessions then made were of benefit to the barons rather than to the landless and dependent classes, and it remained for the third Edward to diminish their power and increase the liberties of the populace.

Law in England during all this period was chiefly a system of oppression, proceeding stage by stage from the highest to the lowest. The revenues of the crown were obtained by extravagant rents, forfeits, taxes, reliefs, fines, aids, and other devices which show the amazing ingenuity of the extortioners. The result was that most tyrannical exactions were made in turn by the feudal lords, and the dependents groaned for six centuries under these lawless yet legalised oppressions. Personal property was at the mercy of the lords, who adopted the most cruel means to enforce their "rights." They, in turn, could be the victim of extortions, as was proved in the case of Roger of Dudley, who was summoned to receive the honour of knighthood in 1233. He found the honour so expensive that he declined to appear, whereupon a writ was issued—" Because Roger de Someri, at the feast of Pentecost last past, has not appeared before the King to be girded with the military girdle, the Sheriff of Worcestershire is hereby commanded to seize on the house of Dudley and all other lands of the said Roger within his jurisdiction, for the King's use; and to keep them with all the cattle found upon them, so that nothing may be moved off without the King's permission." The same Roger had a twelve years' dispute with William de Birmingham touching the service due for the manor of Birmingham, for which the latter was required to perform the service of eight knights' fees, a half and a fourth part, and also to do suit to the court at Dudley once every three weeks. In such wise did these cheftains rule. Another curious piece of law relating to the Dudley lands is told by Leland:—" The lorde Powis, grauntfather that is now, being in a controversy for asawte made upon hym goying to London by the lord Dudeley, Dudeley castelle condesended by entreaty, that his son and heir should mary the olde lorde of Dudleis' daughter." A very amiable method of atoning for personal violence.

The feudal lord had absolute power over his own family, as well as over his dependents, the laws of household government being entirely of

LAW UNDER THE FEUDAL SYSTEM.

his own devising and prompted by his passion, his ignorance, and his wickedness. Robert de Belesme, Earl of Shropshire and of Arundel and Shrewsbury, one of the most powerful and defiant barons of Norman times, tore out the eyes of his own children when they had, in sport, hidden their faces beneath his cloak. He cast his wife in a dungeon, heavily fettered; but every night he sent his servants to drag her to his bed, and in the morning sent her back to her prison. This torture he inflicted upon her to gain money from her family. He disdained to allow his captives in war to be ransomed, but impaled them, men and women, upon stakes. His friends were terrified to approach him, for by way of pleasantry he would engage them in merry chat and suddenly plunge his sword into their sides with a loud laugh. No law could touch this man, and no avenger arose to overcome him. The Warden of the Welsh and English Marches made also his own laws, which were conceived in a spirit of the utmost cruelty. Border foragers, for example, were cast into a dungeon, and subjected to the punishment of having their right hands chopped off with the axe. This prescribed penalty was often aggravated by additional torture or death.

Feudalism was deep-rooted, so deep-rooted that not the enactments of all the Normans and Plantagenets could do more than check its growth and gradually ameliorate its severities. But while some of the old customs were abolished, the bulk of the laws remained based upon the Anglo-Saxon customs, so that as one writer has tersely explained, "the Land Laws and Game Laws are derived from the Normans, the Common Law from the Anglo-Saxons, and almost all our Statute Laws breathe the spirit of pre-Norman England." To this Macaulay refers with ill-disguised scorn in his History:—"Our laws and customs have never been lost in general irreparable ruin. With us the proceedings of the Middle Ages are still valid precedents, and are still cited on the gravest occasions by the most eminent statesmen. . . . Thus in our country the dearest interests of parties have been staked on the results of the researches of antiquaries." The historian, however, does admit that there is compensation for the anomalies which result from this polity. "Other societies possess written constitutions more symmetrical. But no other society has yet succeeded in uniting revolution with prescription, progress with stability, the

LAW UNDER THE FEUDAL SYSTEM. 67

energy of youth with the majesty of immemorial antiquity." That the spirit of olden feudalism should sometimes be found surviving in modern laws is inevitable. Villenage is extinguished, and yet in the very character of certain classes, as well as in the operation of certain laws affecting lands and personal privileges, we see a direct connection between the submission of the bondman in the past to his hereditary master and the readiness of the poor in the present to yield to one in higher station. What struck the philosophic Emerson most, on his visit to England, was that Englishmen should maintain their old customs, repeat the ceremonies of the eleventh century, and consider in so many things that "antiquity of usage is sanction enough." "The Middle Ages," he said, "still lurk in the streets of London."

The stocks and the whipping-post, which stood in front of every castle, were the commonest instruments in use for the punishment of the ceorl and villein who displeased their masters. For the ceorl, who could not quit the land on which he was born, or free himself from slavery, life was particularly hard. He could not absolve himself by money payments, like the rest of his fellow-men, if once he gave offence; while the majority could rob and murder and escape with a fine, the ceorl's slightest defect, real or imagined, was punished with merciless rigour. Tithings and the process of compurgation came to the assistance of other criminals, but the ceorl could appeal to none, and expect neither pity nor aid. Such facts give point to Emerson's dictum that "Castles are proud things, but 'tis safest to be outside them." The villein was in a much happier state than the ceorl. He was free against everybody except his lord, and the criminal code accorded him the same privileges as a free man. The lord was even liable to punishment for killing or mutilating his villein, and the *Mirror of Justice* in the thirteenth century laid down the fact that "the villein is no serf in any sense of the word; he is a free man; his land is a free tenure." But all this is largely comparative, and our estimate of the advantages enjoyed by the villein must depend upon whether we view it by the standards of the time, or by modern standards. At all events, while the ceorl tasted all the bitterness of his serfdom, the adjudged felon in other stations was able to obtain much leniency. The common form of oath or abjuration in King Edward's time was this: "This heare, thou Sir Coroner, that I am a robber and a murderer, and a fellow of our Lord the King of England; and because I have done many such evils in his lande I do abjure the lande of our Lord Edward, and I shall haste me towards the port of ——, which thou hast given me, and that I shall not goe out of the highway, and if I doe, I will that I be taken as a robber and a felon. And that at such a place I will diligentlie seeke for passage, and I will tarrie there but one ebbe and flood, if I can have passage; and unlesse I can have it in such a place I will goe every day into the sea up to my knees, assaying to pass over; and unlesse I can do this within fortie days I will put myselfe again into the Church as a robber and a felon, so God me helpe and his holy judgment." But King Richard showed no disposition to put so much trust in the honour of these gentry, and when setting out for Palestine, he made a law against peculating sailors, which was calculated to dismay them: " Whosoever is convicted of theft shall have his head shaved, melted pitch poured upon it, and the feathers from a pillow shaken over it, that he may be known; and shall be put

on shore on the first land which the ship touches."
This punishment reminds us of a modern
American institution.

The law of "Englishry" deserves a passing
note. It dates back to the time of Canute, and
was continued by the Normans. When Canute
sent away the greater portion of his Danish
troops, "the Witan pledged themselves that the
rest should be safe in life and limb, and that any
Englishman who killed any of them should suffer
punishment. If the murderer could not be discovered, the township or hundred was fined."
The proud and tyrannical Normans used this law
to their own advantage. A mere Englishman
being a vassal, and of no importance, could be
killed with impunity, but it was ordained that
when a man was found killed, and evidence was
not brought to prove that he was English, he
should be held to be a Frenchman, so that a
penalty could be imposed upon the township.
This law of "Englishry" is often illustrated in
old chronicles. Men were found murdered by
the roadside, on heaths, and in woods; the
chronicles state that "no Englishry was proved,"
and the towns were accordingly amerced. The
"Frankpledge" was not so feudal in character,

though it was based upon the principle that "every landless man shall have a lord who shall answer for his appearance in the courts of law." The custom prevailed before the Conquest, ten men forming a "tithing," the members of which were answerable each for others. The present Court Leet is a survival of the system, though in a very modified form.

The feudalism which the Norman barons imposed upon Scotland, and which was unchecked by King William, so that it reproduced all the evils of the ferocious Continental system, was marked by terrible excesses. No institution was more shameful and abhorrent, or so vividly reveals the baseness to which unrestricted feudalism sank, than the horrible depravity of maiden-rights, or *droits de seigneur*. Beaumont and Fletcher founded upon the historic incidents their drama of "The Custom of the Country," and though a few mild attempts have been made to throw doubt upon the facts, there is no question that these domestic tyrannies spread rapidly from Scotland to France and Germany, and took numerous odious forms. Isaac Disraeli, in his "Curiosities," devotes a chapter to the subject, which can scarcely be dealt with in detail in a work appealing to the general reader. The shameful institution was abolished by Malcolm III., who, however, put the matter upon a business basis by ordering that it should be redeemed by a quit-rent. But the lord still considered himself privileged to manifest his authority over his vassals by thrusting his booted leg into the bed of a newly-married couple, or by sousing the bridegroom in a river. The wardships enjoyed by the feudal lords were equally absurd, one of their favourite methods of raising money being to arrange an unsuitable marriage, and on the refusal of the persons to carry out the contract, to claim the revenue of the wards' estate as "forfeit." The feudal lord could sell his vassals as he did his animals, and they were often bartered away with fields and houses. The value of a serf was roughly apprised as four times that of an ox, and he could also be used as "live money."

Mr. Ruskin, in his third letter in "Fors Clavigera," gives an account of the laws promulgated by King Richard, Cœur de Lion, whom he declared to be the truest representative of the British "Squire," under all the significances of that name. The ideal lord was an admixture of the patriarch and the tyrant, and if we examine Richard's legislation, and endeavour to recognise the objects he had in view, we see that with a considerable amount of selfishness he also possessed a real wish to add to the welfare of his people. He simplified and adjusted the weights and measures of the country to put an end to cheating, and he took severe measures "to prevent the extortions of the Jews." If the people would be honest, he was quite willing to do the fighting for them; if they made good cloth, he was ready to see that they got good pay; and when they bought and sold, he was determined that each should give the other good measure. But with much power comes caprice, and the feudal lords too soon forgot the interests of their dependents in serving their own ends. The English barons never made the formal claim of the German barons to rob on the highways in their own territories, though, without asserting the right, they frequently performed the act. A case in point is that of William de Birmingham, who so late as the sixteenth century went out with a hundred men to molest and rob travellers on foot. The ordinary laws were unequal to calling them to account for these misdeeds;

nothing but conquest by battle could have checked them. Besides, there were Lord Palatines whose rule in their own domains was equal to that of the sovereigns, and they could make or abrogate laws at will. These kings *in petto* appointed their own judges and courts, could reverse sentences, pardon at will for any crime, and indict at pleasure. Offences committed in the County Palatine were said to be "against the peace" of the lord, and not against the peace of the king, and it was with a rod of iron that these despots governed the territory allotted to them. Still there was a show of legality in this. It differed from the wanton caprice of Geoffrey of Coventry, who oppressed the inhabitants, was amenable to no law for so doing, but consented to remit the burdensome taxes if his wife would ride naked through the streets. As a specimen of the barbarous humour of these lords, the Godiva story is instructive.

At the end of King Stephen's troublous reign, there were eleven hundred and fifteen castles in England, each of them a centre of power, at that particular time almost absolute. The wise provisions of the Conqueror had to some extent been overcome, and the feudal lords had become so unmanageable that Henry II. found himself compelled to stipulate for the destruction of a number of the strongholds. At the same time he prevented the erection of others except by royal licence, and so began to limit the oppression which had prevailed. We find, too, that in consequence of the frequent over-riding of the common law by men in authority, the monarch reserved to himself more and more of sovereign power, "by which," says Sir Robert Filmer in his famous "Patriarcha"—answered by John Locke in the still more famous treatises on Civil Government—" he did supply the want or correct the rigour of the common law, because the positive law, being grounded upon that which happens for the most part, cannot forsee every particular which time and experience bring forth. Already sundry things do fall out," he continues later, "both in war and peace, that require extraordinary help . . . so that rare matters do grow up meet to be referred to the absolute authority of the prince." We find such a case in the time of Richard II., when, on a question of freehold, the appeal went direct to the king because "of maintenance, oppression, or other outrages the common law cannot have duly her course."

How the lords could avoid and defy the common law is proved by two curious instances in the history of the Dudleys, the family previously referred to. Lord Edward Dudley, in 1592, had a dispute with the neighbouring Lyttelton family, and raising some 150 persons, he went one night and stole all the cattle on the latter's estate. Lyttelton obtained judgment against Dudley, who was ordered to return the cattle, but he posted his servants at the gates, and bade them cut the bailiffs to pieces. Lyttelton then armed sixty men and took the cattle back by force; Dudley armed 700 men to fetch them back and kill them. For this offence the nobleman and eighty followers were indicted, but by one means and another the proceedings were made to last four years, and then an agreement was entered into by the parties. Lord Edward's son, Ferdinando, was the hero of the next exploit. He purchased the property of an oppressed widow, named Martha Grovenor, for £1200, but only paid £100. She sued him in the Exchequer for the remainder, and obtained judgment for the balance. No notice was taken of this. The following year the widow obtained a second decree, and this again was ignored. His lordship

LAW UNDER THE FEUDAL SYSTEM. 77

was next called upon for costs, and this led him to make an effort to compromise the matter. He entered into an agreement to pay all arrears and costs, but, having done so much, refused to fulfil his obligations. An execution of ejectment was then levied against his lordship. This he avoided for nine years, and it was only twelve years after negotiations had begun that the widow was able to obtain her dues.

A very brief glance at Continental feudalism and its influence upon statute law may now be given. It enables us to mark some of the differences between the English and the foreign systems, the one with its restrictions and the other all-powerful. In the eleventh century, all France and the German Empire were one vast feudal possession. The powers of the lords have been classed by the historian Hallam as follows— First, the right of coining money; second, that of waging private war; third, exemption from all public tributes except the feudal aids; fourth, freedom from legislative control; and fifth, the exclusive exercise of original judicature in their dominions. It is easy to perceive how, with these initial powers conceded, the seigneurs were enabled to make themselves the veritable masters of the kingdom. In Germany the lawlessness of the barons became as proverbial as did their cruelty towards their slaves. The whole country was divided up into territories over which the feudal chiefs reigned as absolute and despotic kings. Nor is the spirit of feudalism in that country yet extinct, for, unlike France, it has not had its bloody revolt against "aristocrats." No one can have travelled in Germany and seen the castle towering high on crag or rock, and the diminutive houses scattered about its base, without realising at a glance how the chieftains and their serfs lived in the old days. In Germany the feudal system was seen at its strongest and its worst, and law was paralysed while the men of lust and blood were supreme in their own dominions. Austria has a similar story to tell of barbarity towards serfs, and the abrogation of law by powerful chieftains. But it is remarkable that in Russia, where the feudal spirit still most strongly survives, and is marked by many excesses utterly repugnant to the feeling and customs of the times, the earliest attempts to establish a feudal system were quelled by the princes. In this land, where a mistress might, until recently, have her maid whipped to death

LAW UNDER THE FEUDAL SYSTEM.

for dropping a teacup, or for any other trivial offence, real or imagined, where again it was taken for granted that

> "A Count carbonadoes
> His ignorant serfs with the knout,"

feudalism, once instituted, deepened its hold with the progress of years. While there was no law for the lower classes, save that dictated by the caprice of their masters, there were special exemptions and priveleges for the noble and wealthy. The Russian lords pay no taxes, and they retain, in almost undiminished force, that power to abuse, insult, and destroy the peasantry which was possessed by the *ancienne noblesse* of France before the Revolution. Mr. Morley Roberts, in one of his Russian historical sketches, relates that not long ago a noble threw a Hebrew into a dungeon for an offence, and a week later asked his jäger what had become of him. "Oh," said the fellow with a laugh, "he made so much noise that I shot him."

The state of Bohemia from the ninth to the fourteenth century shows to what deplorable depths a race may sink under an unrestrained and licentious feudalism. The Bohemian nobles practically abolished the marriage laws, and in addition to oppressing their dependents, frequently sold them into slavery. When St. Adalbert endeavoured to effect a reformation, he found every impediment put in his way, and his wishes openly defied. He had a horror of bloodshed, and preached the hatefulness of murder. By way of response, a man, whose wife had been put in a nunnery to save her from his brutality, was dragged out and butchered in the streets. Adalbert had to wait long before he could influence these men who, secure in their castles, could indulge their rapacity without fear of punishment. Reforms, effected in the tenth century, however, were not permanent, and in the twelfth century the nobles had succeeded in converting the local assembly, with its power of appointing judges, to their own uses. Mr. Edmund Maurice, in his history of Bohemia, relates that the nobles began to secure the judgeships for themselves, and then sold or bequeathed the offices to heirs. They thus made the appointments a means of tyranny and a source of profit, and with the money acquired purchased the lands of freemen. Others, owing to the unpopularity of the local tribunals, strengthened the power of their own feudal

LAW UNDER THE FEUDAL SYSTEM. 81

courts, and again reduced their dependents to abject slavery.

"The coolness," says Mr. Maurice, "with which many of the grants of land transferred workmen of various kinds as mere appendages of fields and fishponds, is in itself a proof of the degraded position to which the peasant class had been reduced; and the fact that military service seemed one of the few means of escaping from serfdom, led the peasants to favour those wars which in the end increased their misery." Eventually King Wenceslas, famed in ballad, and still more famed in Bohemian history, came to the rescue, and ordained "that no baron or noble of the land shall have power in the city of Brünn, or shall do any violence in it, or shall detain anyone, without the license and proclamation of the judge of the city."

The wide survey we have taken enables a fair estimate to be made of the state of the law in Europe when the castle was the court of justice, and the baron was the judge. England alone of all Europeon countries seems to have been able to place a check upon the more flagrant abuses, and in later times of reform to have

6

succeeded, while abolishing what was essentially evil in the system, in retaining whatever of it was of worth. Whether there be still laws too deeply impressed with feudal ideas for modern acceptance is a question for legislators to consider.

The Manor and Manor Law.

By England Howlett.

EVERYTHING relating to the manor reminds us forcibly of the baron of olden days, with his little territory, in which he was practically a king. Estates in copyhold are essentially distinct both in their origin and in their nature from those of freehold estates. Copyhold lands are holden by *copy* of court roll, that is to say, the muniments of the title to such lands are *copies* of the roll or book in which an account is kept of the proceedings in the *court* of the manor to which the lands belong. For it must be remembered that all copyhold lands belong to and are parcel of some manor. An estate in copyhold is not a freehold; but, according to construction of law, merely an estate *at the will of the lord* of the manor, at whose will copyhold estates are expressed to be holden. Copyholds are also said to be holden *according to the custom* of the manor to which they belong, for custom is of course the life and being of copyholds.

We must remember that in former days, a baron, or great lord, becoming possessed of a large tract of land, granted part of it to freemen for estates in fee simple. Part of the land he reserved to himself, and this formed the demesnes of the manor, properly so called : other parts of the land he granted out to his villeins, or slaves, permitting them, as an act of pure grace and favour, to enjoy such lands at his pleasure ; but sometimes enjoining, in return for such favour, the performance of certain agricultural services, such, for instance, as ploughing the demesne, carting the manure, and other such servile work. The lands remaining after this parcelling out, generally the poorest, formed the waste lands of the manor, over which rights of commons were enjoyed by the tenants. In this way arose a manor, of which it will be seen the tenants formed two classes, the freeholders and the villeins. Now for each of these classes a separate court was held—for the freeholders a Court Baron ; for the villeins another called a Customary Court. In the former court the suitors were the judges ; in the latter the lord only, or his steward.

THE MANOR AND MANOR LAW. 85

In some manors the villeins were allowed to have life interests, but these grants were not extended so as to admit any of their children. Hence arose copyholds for life. Again, in other manors a much greater degree of liberality was shown by the lords; and on the death of a tenant, the lord permitted his eldest son, or indeed sometimes all his sons, or sometimes the youngest only, and afterwards other relations to succeed him by way of heirship; for which privilege, however, the payment of a fine was usually required on the admittance of the heir to the tenancy. Frequently it happened that the course of descent of estates of freehold was chosen as the model for such inheritances; but in many cases dispositions of the most capricious kind were adopted by the lord of the manor, and in course of time actually became the custom of the manor. And thus it was that copyholds of inheritance arose. Again, if a villein tenant wished to part with his own parcel of land to some other of his fellows, the lord would allow him to *surrender* or yield up again the land, and then, on the payment of a fine, would indulgently *admit* as his tenant, on the same terms, the other, to whose use and in whose favour the surrender had been made. Thus arose the method now prevalent at the present day, of conveying copyholds by *surrender* into the hands of the lord of the manor to the use of the purchaser, and the subsequent admittance of the latter. By long custom and continued indulgence that which at first was a pure favour gradually grew up into a right, and thus it came to pass that the will of the lord, which had of course originated the custom, came at last to be controlled by it. *

The rise of the copyholder from a state of uncertainty to certainty of tenure appears to have been very gradual. Britton, who wrote in the reign of Edward I., thus describes this tenure under the name of Villeinage. "Villeinage is to hold part of the demesnes of any lord entrusted to hold at his will by villein services to improve for the advantage of the lord." And he further adds that "In manors of ancient demesne there were pure villeins of blood and of tenure, who might be ousted of their tenements at the will of their lord."

In the reign of Edward III. a case occured in which the entry of a lord on his copyholder was adjudged lawful, *because he did not do his services,*

* Williams' "Real Property Law."

by which he broke the custom of the manor, which seems to show that even at that time the lord could not have ejected his tenant without a cause. And later, in the reign of Edward IV., the judges gave to copyholders a certainty of tenure by allowing them an action of trespass on ejectment by their lords without just cause. "Now," says Sir Edward Coke, "copyholders stand upon a sure ground; now they weigh not their lord's displeasure; they shake not at every sudden blast of wind; they eat, drink, and sleep securely; only having a special care of the main chance, namely, to perform carefully what duties and services soever their tenure doth exact and custom doth require; then let lord frown, the copyholder cares not, knowing himself safe."

In the present day a copyholder has as good a title as a freeholder; in some respects a better; for all the transactions relating to the conveyance of copyholds are entered on the court rolls of the manor, and thus a record is preserved of the title of all the tenants.

Since the passing of the statute of *Quia Emptores*, 18 Edward I., it has not been lawful to create a tenure of an estate in fee simple; so that every manor bears date at least as far back as that reign; to this rule the few seignories, which may have been subsequently created by the king's tenants in capite, form the only exception.

The name "manor" is of Norman origin, but the estate to which it was given existed, in its essential character, long before the Conquest; it received a new name as the shire also did, but neither the one nor the other was created by this change. The local jurisdiction of the thegns who had grants of sac and soc, or who exercised judicial functions amongst their free neighbours, were identical with the manorial jurisdictions of the new owners.

Although long continued custom has now rendered copyholders quite independent of the will of the lords, yet all copyholds, properly so called, are still expressly stated, in the court rolls of manors, to be holden at the will of the lord; and, more than this, estates in copyholds are still liable to some of the incidents of mere estates at will.

In ancient times the law laid great stress on the feudal possession or seisin of lands, and this possession could only be had by the holder of an estate of freehold, that is, an estate sufficiently important to belong to a free man. Now, as we have seen, copyholders in ancient times belonged to the class of villeins or bondsmen, and held, at the will of the lord, lands of which the lord himself was alone feudally possessed. The lands held by the copyholders still remained part and parcel of the lord's manor; and the freehold of these lands still continued vested in the lord; and this is the case at the present day with regard to all copyholds. The lord of the manor is actually seised of all the lands in the possession of his copyhold tenants.

The lord, having the legal fee simple in the copyhold lands comprised in his manor, possesses all the rights incident to such an estate, controlled only by the custom of the manor, which is now the tenant's safeguard. Thus he possesses a right to all the mines and minerals under the land, and also to all timber growing on the surface, and this even though the timber may have been planted by the tenant. However, it must be borne in mind that these rights are somewhat interfered with by the rights which long continued custom has given to the tenants, for the lord cannot come upon the lands to open his mines, or to cut his timber, without the copyholder's leave.

A copyholder cannot commit any waste, either voluntary, by opening mines, cutting down timber or pulling down buildings; or permissive, by neglecting to repair. For the land, with all that is under it or upon it, belongs to the lord of the manor; the tenant has nothing but a customary right to enjoy the occupation; and if he should in any way exceed this right, a cause of forfeiture to his lord would at once accrue. *

By the customs of manors, on every change of tenancy, whether by death, sale, or otherwise, fines of more or less amount become payable to the lord. By the customs of some manors the fine payable was anciently arbitrary; but now in modern times, fines, even when arbitrary by custom, are restrained to two years' improved value of the land after deducting quit rents.

In some manors a fine is due on the change of the lord; but in this case the change must always be by act of God, and not by any act of the party.

The tenure of an estate in copyholds involves an oath of fealty from the tenant, and together also with suit to the customary court of the manor. Another incident of the tenure, and this

* Williams' "Real Property Law."

THE MANOR AND MANOR LAW. 91

sometimes a very profitable one, is the escheat to the lord on failure of heirs.

Before the abolition of forfeiture for treason and felony, the lord of a copyholder had a great advantage over the lord of a freeholder in this respect, that, whilst freehold lands in fee simple were forfeited to the crown by the treason of the tenant, the copyholds of a traitor escheated to the lord of the manor of which they were held.

One of the most curious incidents of the tenure is the right of the lord, on the death of a tenant, to seize the tenant's best beast, horse, or other chattel under the name of a heriot. Now it would appear that heriots were introduced into England by the Danes. The heriot of a military tenant was his arms and habiliments of war, which belonged to the lord for the purpose of equipping his successor. And it would seem that in analogy to this purely feudal custom, the lords of manors usually expected that the best beast or other chattel of each tenant, whether he were a freeman or a villein, should on his death be left to them. In old wills of copyholders we constantly find this legacy to the lord of the manor the first bequest mentioned: in fact the tenant really making a bounty of what was actually an obligation. In cases where the tenant died intestate the heriot of the lord was taken in the first place out of his effects, unless indeed the lord seized the whole of the goods, which not unfrequently happened in days before custom had so completely controlled the rights of the lord, and at the same time protected the interests of the tenant. Heriots survive to this day in many manors, a true badge of the ancient servility of the tenure. Now, however, the right of the lord is confined to such a chattel as the custom of the manor, grown into a law, will permit him to take; and in most cases the heriot consists not of a chattel at all, but merely of a money payment.

The mode in which copyhold land is transferred from one person to another still retains much of the primitive simplicity of bygone ages. The copyholder personally surrenders the lands into the hands of the lord, generally through his steward, and this surrender is evidenced by the delivery of some article varying according to the custom of the particular manor: in some manors the surrender is effected by the delivery of a rod, in others of a straw, and again in others by a glove. The surrender having been duly effected, the purchaser is admitted, and the various

THE MANOR AND MANOR LAW. 93

documents used are all entered upon the court rolls of the manor. The steward is the person who makes the entries on the court rolls, and they are kept in his custody, but subject however to the right of the tenants to inspect them. The steward also usually presides at the copyhold courts of the manor.

A special custom is required to entitle the wife of a copyholder to any interest in her husband's lands on his death intestate. Where such a custom does exist the wife's interest is termed her *freebench*, and it consists generally of a life interest in one-third part of the lands of which the husband died possessed. Freebench in most manors differs from the ancient right of dower in this most important particular, that whilst the widow could claim her dower out of all the freehold lands which her husband actully possessed at any time during the marriage, the right to freebench does not in general attach until the actual death of the husband, and of course may be defeated by a devise of lands by the husband's will. From this it will be seen that freebench is no impediment to free alienation by the husband of his copyholds without any consent on the part of his wife. To this general rule, however, the manor of Cheltenham forms an important exception; for by the custom of this manor the widow's freebench attaches in the same way as the ancient right of dower did on all the land of copyhold tenure, of which the husband at any time during the marriage had been possessed.

Centuries have robbed the manor of much of its importance; most of the honour and prestige has decayed which once surrounded the lord, his power has become controlled by long continued custom, so that the copyhold tenants are practically independent of him, and have as good a title to their lands as freeholders. Little remains beyond the most prominent of the old formalities, which at one time gave dignity and importance to the lord of the manor and his court. Most of the dealings with copyhold land are now effected out of court, and although the courts are still held at the customary periods, they are for the most part an empty formality, their glamour gone, yet still possessing an especial interest of their own as evidence of the surviving of ancient customs, which have practically remained unchanged through the roll of centuries.

Ancient Tenures.

By England Howlett.

PRACTICALLY all the landed property in England is, by the policy of our laws, supposed to be granted by, dependent upon, and holden of some superior lord, in consideration of certain services to be rendered to such lord by the possessor of this property, and the terms or manner of their possession is therefore called a *tenure*. Thus all the land in the kingdom is supposed to be held, mediately or immediately, of the sovereign who is consequently styled the lord or lady *paramount*.

All tenures being thus derived, or supposed to be derived, from the sovereign, those who held directly under such sovereign, and in right of the crown and dignity, were called tenants *in capite*, or *in chief*, which was the most honourable species of tenure, although at the same time it subjected the tenants to far greater and more burthensome services than the inferior tenures did, and this distinction ran through all the different sorts of tenure. William I., and other feudal sovereigns, although they made large and numerous grants of land, always reserved a rent or certain annual payments, which were collected by the sheriffs of the counties in which the lands lay, to show that they still retained the *dominium directum* in themselves.

With our ancestors the most honourable and highly esteemed species of tenure was that by knight service, and this was purely and entirely a military tenure, being, in fact, the result of the feudal establishment in England. Now to make a tenure by knight service, a determinate quantity of land was necessary, which was called a knight's fee, *feodum militare*; the measure of which in 3 Edward I., was estimated at twelve ploughlands, and its value (although it varied with the times) in the reigns of Edward I. and Edward II. was stated at £20 per annum. The knight who held this proportion of land was bound to attend his lord to the wars for forty days in every year, if called upon so to do, which attendance was his rent or service for the land he claimed to hold. If, however, he held only half a knight's fee, he was only bound to attend his lord twenty days, and so on in proportion. This tenure of knight service drew with it several consequences as inseparably incident to the tenure in chivalry, and one of the most profitable, and, at the same time, arbitrary of these was marriage. This incident called marriage was the right which the lord possessed of disposing of his infant wards in matrimony, at their peril of forfeiting to him, in case of their refusing a suitable match, a sum of money equal to the value of the marriage; that is, what the suitor was willing to pay down to the lord as the price of marrying his ward; and double the market value was to be forfeited, if the ward presumed to marry without the consent of the lord.

The personal attendance rendered necessary by knight service growing troublesome and inconvenient in many respects, the tenants found means of compounding for it; first, by sending others in their stead, and then in process of time making a pecuniary satisfaction to the lord in lieu of it. This pecuniary satisfaction at last came to be levied by assessments at so much for every knight's fee; the first time this appears to have been done was in 5 Henry II., on account of his expedition to Toulouse; but it soon became so universal that personal attendance fell quite into disuse. From this period we find, from our ancient histories, that when the kings went to war, they levied scutages on their tenants, that is, on all the landowners of the Kingdom, to defray their expenses, and to pay for the hire of troops.

These assessments, in the time of Henry II., seem to have been made in a most arbitrary manner, and entirely at the king's will and pleasure. The prerogative became, indeed, abused to such an extent, that at last it became a matter of national clamour, and King John was obliged to consent by his *Magna Carta*, that no scutage should be imposed without the consent of Parliament. But this clause was omitted in the Charter of Henry III., where we only find that scutages, or escuage, should be taken as they were used to be taken in the time of Henry II.; that is, in a reasonable and moderate manner. Yet afterwards, by statute 25 Edward I., and many subsequent statutes, it was again provided, that the king should take no aids or tasks but by the common assent of the realm; hence it was held that scutage, or escuage, could not be levied except with the consent of Parliament; such scutages being indeed the groundwork of all

ANCIENT TENURES.

succeeding subsidies, and the land tax of later times.

It will easily be seen that with the degenerating of knight service, or personal military duty into a pecuniary assessment, all the advantages were destroyed, and nothing in fact remained but the hardships. Instead of having a national militia, composed of barons, knights, and gentlemen, bound by their interests and their honour to defend the king and country, the whole system of military tenures tended to nothing else but a wretched means of raising money to pay an army of occasional mercenaries. At length the military tenures, with all their heavy appendages were destroyed at one blow by statute, 12 Charles II., C. 24, which enacts "that the courts of wards and liveries, and all wardships, liveries, primer seisins, and ousterlemains, values and forfeitures of marriage, by reason of any tenure of the king or others, be totally taken away. And that all fines for alienation, tenures by homage, knight service, and escuage, and also aids for marrying the daughter, or knighting the son, and all tenures of the king *in capite*, be likewise taken away. And that all sorts of tenures, held of the king or others, be turned into free and common socage;

save only tenures in frank almoign, copyholds, and the honorary services of grand serjeanty."

Another ancient tenure was that by *Grand Serjeanty,* whereby the tenant was bound, instead of serving the king generally in the wars, to do some special honorary service for the king in person; as to carry his banner, his sword, or the like; or to be his butler, champion, or other officer at his coronation. Tenure by *cornage* was a species of grand serjeanty, being a grant of land upon condition that the tenant was to wind a horn when the Scots or other enemies entered the land, in order to warn the king's subjects.

The tenure of petit serjeanty bears a great resemblance to the tenure of grand serjeanty; for as the one is a personal service, so the other is a rent or render, both tending to some purpose relative to the king's person. Petit serjeanty as defined by Littleton, consists in holding lands of the king, by service of rendering to him annually some small implement of war, as a bow, a sword, a lance, an arrow, or the like. This, of course, is but socage in effect, for it is no personal service, but a certain rent. The tenure by which the grants to the Duke of Marlborough and the Duke of Wellington, for their great military services to the country, are held, are of this kind, each rendering a small flag or ensign annually, which is deposited in Windsor Castle. Bury House (New Forest), the property of Sir Charles Mill, Bart., is held by the tenure of presenting the king whenever he enters the New Forest with a brace of milk-white greyhounds. A breed of these dogs is preserved by the family in readiness. King George III. received dogs in recognition of this tenure in 1789, and the incident is the subject of one of Lawrence's pictures.

In Beckwith's edition of Blount's "Fragmenta Antiquitatis," the following tenure is inserted from the "Black Book of Hereford."—"The tenants at Hampton Bishop, in the county of Hereford, were to get yearly six horse loads of rods or wattels, in the Hay Wood, near Hereford, and bring them to Hereford to make booths (or hurdles to pen sheep in) at the fair when they should be required; and for every load of the said rods they were to be allowed a halfpenny at the fairs."

This tenure would appear to relate to one particular fair only, and not to all the fairs formerly held at Hereford. The particular fair is supposed to have been the one beginning on

May 19th, and commonly called the nine-days' fair, from the circumstance of its continuing for that length of time. From time immemorial this fair was proclaimed, with certain formalities, by the Bishop of Hereford's bailiff, or his deputy, the tolls of the fair belonging to one or both of these officers. During the continuance of the fair, the Bishop's bailiff superseded the Mayor of Hereford as acting magistrate, the fair being held in a street opposite the Bishop's palace.

Brienston, in Dorsetshire, was held in grand serjeanty by a curious jocular tenure, viz. :—by finding a man to go before the king's army for forty days when he should make war in Scotland (some records say in Wales) bareheaded and barefooted, in his shirt, and linen drawers, holding in one hand a bow, and in the other an arrow without feathers.*

The Dukes of Athol hold the Blair Athol estate by the tenure of presenting a white rose to the sovereign whenever he visits them there.

Land was frequently held by the tenure of protecting the church property in times of war. Scott tells us how the Bishop of Durham gave

* Southey's Common Place Book, 4th Series, 1851, p. 175.

ANCIENT TENURES.   103

lands to the Danish Count, Witikind, to be held by this tenure. The story is not true, but the tenure is ;

> Broad lands he gave him on Tyne and Wear,
> To be held of the Church by bridle and spear ;
> Part of Monkwearmouth, of Tynedale part,
> To better his will and soften his heart.
> *Harold the Dauntless.*
> Canto i., IV.

The tenure of ancient demesne exists in those manors, and in those only, which belonged to the crown in the reigns of Edward the Confessor and William the Conqueror, and in Domesday Book are called *Terræ Regis Edwardi.* The tenants are freeholders and possessed certain privileges, the chief of which was a right to sue and be sued only in their lord's court.

Another kind of ancient tenure, still subsisting, is the tenure of frankalmoign, or free alms, and this is the tenure by which the lands of the church are for the most part held. This tenure is expressly excepted from the statute, 12 Charles II., by which the other ancient tenures were destroyed. It has no peculiar incidents, the tenants not being bound even to do fealty to the lords, because, as Littleton says, the prayers and other divine services of the tenants are better for the lords than any doing of fealty. As the church is a body having perpetual existence, there is, moreover, no chance of any escheat. By this tenure almost all the monasteries and religious houses held their lands. It was an old Saxon tenure; and continued under the Norman revolution, through the great respect that was shewn to religion and religious men in ancient times. This too, no doubt, is the reason that tenants in frankalmoign were discharged from all other services except the repairing of highways, building castles, and repelling invasions; just in fact as the Druids, among the Ancient Britons, had similar privileges. The tenure being purely spiritual, the lord had no remedy for neglect by distress or otherwise, but merely a complaint to the ordinary to correct it.

One of the most interesting tenures is that of Borough English. There are a great number of manors throughout the country in which this tenure prevails; they are not however confined to one county or one district. Borough English is the right of succession of the youngest son, instead of the eldest, to real estate in case of intestacy, but the custom is not always the same;

it differs in different manors. In some it is confined to the sons only, and if there should be no son the estate is shared equally amongst all the daughters. In other manors, principally Sussex, the youngest daughter inherits. Again, there are cases to be found where if there be no children, the youngest brother inherits, and in others it goes according to the rules of the common law. There are, moreover, places in which the copyhold land only is Borough English, while the freehold is held by the ordinary tenure, and in others the freehold and copyhold alike follow the Borough English custom.

The area over which this Borough English tenure prevails is an exceedingly wide one. It is found in nearly every part of Europe, except perhaps Italy and Spain—in Germany, Hungary, the Ural mountains, and in Asia as far as the borders of China. Many attempts have been made to explain the custom. Littleton suggests that the youngest son, by reason of his tender age, is not so capable as the rest of his brethren to help himself. It is possible the origin may have come to us from the Tartars, amongst whom this custom of descent to the youngest son also prevails. That nation is composed almost entirely of shepherds and herdsmen, and the elder sons, as soon as they are capable of leading a pastoral life, migrate from their father with a certain allotment of cattle, and go to seek a new habitation. And thus we find that, among many other northern nations, it was the custom for all the sons, but one, to migrate from the father, which one became his heir.

The tenure of Gavelkind prevails principally in the County of Kent. It is universally known what struggles the Kentish men made to preserve their ancient liberties, and with how much success those struggles were attended. It seems fair therefore, to conclude that this custom was a part of those liberties, agreeably to the general opinion, that Gavelkind, before the Norman Conquest, was the general custom of the realm. The distinguishing properties of this tenure are various; some of the principal are these: 1. The tenant is of age sufficient to alienate his estate by feoffment at the age of fifteen. 2. There never was any escheat in case of an attainder and execution for felony; their maxim being "the father to the bough, the son to the plough." 3. In most places, the tenant had the power of devising his lands by will, before the statute for that purpose was made. 4. The lands descend not to the eldest, youngest, or any one son only, but to all the sons together. This last incident is, of course, the most important affecting the tenure, and not only this, but also the most interesting, in that, like Borough English, it prevails to the present day. True it is that certain lands in Kent, once Gavelkind, have been made descendable according to the rules of the common law, by special statutes; however, these statutes only affect a very small portion of the county.

Gavelkind and Borough English, being customs already acknowledged by the law, need not be specially pleaded; it is sufficient to show that the lands are affected and regulated by the same; but all other private customs must be pleaded.

The ancient Barons of Buccleuch, both from feudal splendour and from their frontier situation, retained in their household at Branksome a number of gentlemen of their own name, who held lands from their chief for the military service of watching and guarding his castle.

<pre>
        Nine and twenty knights of fame
        Hung their shields in Branksome Hall
</pre>

Nine and twenty squires of name
   Brought them their steeds from bower to stall.
Nine and twenty yeomen tall
   Waited duteous on them all.
They were all knights of metal true,
   Kinsmen to the bold Buccleuch.
                "Lay of the Last Minstrel."—Scott.
                     Canto i., III.

Laws of the Forest.

By Edward Peacock, f.s.a.

THE subject of "The Laws of the Forest" and of the wild things which have their homes therein, both in our own island and elsewhere, has been a matter of discussion for ages; but very little has been written thereon which is of much service, except to legal specialists. It is, indeed, one of those difficult subjects which is hardly possible to make interesting to those whose thoughts range in the present rather than in the past.

There can be no doubt whatever, that from the birth of the human race, long ere we can trace our history back in written documents, the killing of animals has been a sport as well as a means of procuring food; both these may be considered, whatever certain dreamers may aver to the contrary, as among the necessities of human life. We cannot be quite certain whether the stone axes, hammers, and spears, of which we see such numbers in our museums, were wrought in anticipation of the delights of the chase, or whether they were simply, what may be called, the tools of the primæval butcher; but, knowing as we do, the contempt in which every man at the present hour is held, who having wealth and leisure enough to indulge in what is called "sport," abstains from amusing himself in some form of slaughter, we may well believe that our palæolithic predecessors, however empty the larder might be, would try to impose on themselves that what they did was done to amuse themselves, as a manly exercise, not a stern necessity. In confirmation of this, we must call mind that there have been found several weapons with the reindeer and other animals carved, or perhaps it would be better to say scratched, upon them with a high degree of pictorial excellence; we may therefore infer that amusement, as well as appetite, occupied the minds of those early artists, who so deftly represented the creatures on whom they waged war. Had they merely been regarded as things to be eaten, such as the tinned meats we now buy from the provision merchant, they would never have been held worthy of artistic treatment.

One of the oldest proverbs that have come down

LAWS OF THE FOREST. 111

to us, if indeed it be not the very oldest, is that wherein we are told something

> "Of Nimrod the founder
> Of empire and chace,
> Who made the woods wonder
> And quake for their race."

That he was the first of the great hunters is a dream of Lord Byron's, not in any way countenanced by Holy Scriptures, or any of the old authorities. We are simply told in Genesis that Nimrod was a son of Cush, and that "He began to be a mighty one in the earth. He was a mighty hunter before the Lord. Wherefore it is said, even as Nimrod the mighty hunter before the Lord."* The precise meaning of this has been questioned. It most likely signifies that Nimrod was the first person who organised those mighty hunting expeditions, which were so famous in the days of the great Oriental despotisms. From these tyrants it is probable that the Forest Laws of Mediæval Europe had their origin. In the sculptures that have been unearthed in the dead cities of the East, hunting scenes of great magnificence are not uncommon, nor are they unknown in Egypt, where, however,

* Chapter x., verses 8 and 9.

the capture of fish was the more common sport, as the Nile may be said to have been at every man's door.

That Forest Laws of some kind or other existed in these far-off times may be accepted as certain, and we may take it for granted, when we call to mind the general legislation then in force, that they were terribly cruel according to our modern ideas, but we can at present only arrive at these conclusions by inference.

When Rome became the mistress of the world, we know that in many parts of the empire the wild creatures were rigorously preserved, but we do not think that they were often hunted by their owners. Such was rather the duty of freed men and slaves. Those which were fit for food were preserved as delicacies for the table, but the larger beasts, such as the lion, the tiger, the bear, the lynx, and perhaps even the wild cat, were reserved for the sports of the amphitheatre. Amphitheatres were much more common than is usually supposed. In a few places their remains exist still, but most of them have perished, serving as quarries for stone during the whole of the Middle Ages, and in Mohammedan lands to a much more modern period, perhaps even to the present day. We are not sure that any list of them has been preserved, or could now be compiled, but they were so numerous throughout the empire that the possession of wild beasts on the immense estates of the Roman patricians must have been a great source of wealth to their owners. The Roman nobles did not care for field-sports as the northern nations did. A feeling or instinct of this kind dies hard. At the present day the Italian cares much less for such amusements than the Englishman, the German, or the inhabitants of northern France. Virgil, who represents more fully than any other heathen poet, the feelings of the better sort of Romans of his own time, says, attributing the words to another, but evidently speaking his own thoughts :—

"Above aught else let the woods be dear to me."*

This was, however, not for the sake of the slaughter that might be perpetrated therein, but on account of their many beauties and the grateful shade which they afforded. Virgil was in many respects a modern in his love of scenery, though we doubt whether snow-clad mountains and craggy heights would have appealed to him as they have

* Ecl. II., line 62.

done to us during the short time that has elapsed since we have been able to see them without discomfort.

When the Roman Empire was in the zenith of its glory, there does not seem to have been in Gaul or Britain any vast stretches of forest. The country was no doubt well wooded when we compare it with the France or England of to-day, for during the last two hundred years trees have been wantonly destroyed, to the great injury of agriculture as well as local beauty, for the sake of supplying land-owners with ready money. Long continued wars have also desolated the national forests for the sake of supplying timber to the shipbuilder.

After the various invasions which desolated so many parts of the Roman Empire, large portions of Gaul reverted to a state of nature. Towns and villages were burned, their inhabitants slaughtered, or scattered far away from their homes. A picturesque account of what followed is given in Montalembert's *Les Moines d'Occident*, from which we gather that much of Gaul had reverted to a state of nature, such as it was in ere civilisation had made its first incursions on the untamed wilderness. The lives of the early Gallic saints, found scattered through the many volumes of the *Acta Sanctorum*, bear the like testimony, as do many parts of the old romances, the scenes of which so often lie in the trackless forest.

In England, things may not have been quite so woeful. The population, we believe, never became so scanty as in Eastern Gaul. It is still a matter of controversy whether here the native folk were slaughtered or driven into the mountains of Wales, or whether the greater part of them were made bondmen. We hold the latter opinion, but the whole subject is beset with great difficulties. However this may be, it is quite certain that the population was very much reduced; many wide districts, which had been carefully cultivated by the Roman settlers, or natives who had adopted their manners, were laid waste. The picturesque villas, with their adjoining peasant homesteads, were all gone—burnt with fire,—and woodland, scrub, or mere sandy desolation supplied the place of the adjoining pleasure-grounds, farms, and pastures. One of these desolate tracts named Andredsweald stretched from Kent to the Hampshire Downs, at some points almost touching the Thames. Another great forest appears to have extended from a point a little to the north of

London, till it reached the forests of Rockingham and Sherwood. The great level of Hatfield Chace seems to have been a spur of this, if not so, they were but separated by a narrow stretch of cultivated land from the forest itself. Deer were plentiful on Hatfield Chace until the reign of Charles the First. They even continued to exist longer on the eastern side of the Trent, on a long and narrow belt of scrub which extended from Morton, near Gainsburgh, to the point where the Trent falls into the Humber. An ancestor of our own, who died as recently as 1758, was accustomed to hunt them there. As well as these larger forests, the whole land was dotted over with places once the sites of Roman dwellings, but which now had become either mere wastes, or woodlands covered with tall timber trees, interspersed with the elder, the nut, the thorn, the birch, the maple, and the alder. In some places the yew and the holly were abundant also, but they seem to have flourished only in widely separated patches.

The Saxon and the Danish conquests came about gradually, and the country was in so disturbed a state that it was impossible for rigid Forest Laws to be enacted, or even if

LAWS OF THE FOREST. 117

written on parchment to be put in force. Besides this, the Saxon and Danish leaders were of a different character from their Norman successors. A vague memory still haunted them of the free life once lived in Germany and Scandinavia; a life as different as can well be imagined from that of modern democracy, but still one in which every thrall, bondman, and slave had certain well ascertained rights, which were under the protection of the State and the Church.

Thus it came to pass that there were in almost every district stretches of forest land, which were, in a great degree, open to the people, where men could fell timber for their dwellings and slaughter animals for food; though even before the Norman Conquest had come as a shadow on the liberties of Englishmen, there is reason for thinking that forestal-rights had become, in name at least, a privilege of the king and his great theïgns.

The Norman Forest Law was of a similar character to that which William's forefathers had enforced in Normandy. The country, which we have for ages known as France, was, in earlier times, broken up into many provinces, and it was only by a slow process that it became one. Each of these provinces had a Forest Law of its own. When the Normans settled in the goodly land which they called after themselves, they retained the customs which they found there. When William transferred the laws of his old duchy to his new kingdom, it could, at the first, only be by an act of favour that anyone could kill a beast of chase except himself or his retainers. This from the nature of things did not last long. William never could have intended to retain the whole of the vast territories which the victory of Senlac had given him in his own possession. He divided the kingdom among his chief tenants—tenants *in capite*,—and to these great men, with some slight exceptions, he handed over all forestal rights which existed in their domains, the king retaining to himself for his own pleasure, and as a mark of dignity, some great forests, which for ages have remained in royal hands.

Notwithstanding certain Danish and Saxon charters, it has always been traditionally held that our Forest Laws come from William the First, and this is substantially true, though objections to the statement might be taken. It would not be unsafe to say that no one but the Conqueror could have enforced so drastic a

LAWS OF THE FOREST.

regulation. As the Bishop of Oxford has so truly said, "The King made and kept good peace. The Dane-geld and the Forest-Law were not too much to pay for the escape from private war and feudal disruption."* It is true that William had desolated large tracts of land to make them serve him for the chase; the crime was terrible, though exaggerated by modern historians; but he had many noble qualities, so that those who had not personally suffered were willing to overlook the evil. With his son, William the Red, the Forest Laws became unbearable, and were hated by baron and villain alike.

He was one of the worst kings which ever disgraced the English throne. In a deeply religious age he was wantonly opposed to all godliness. Alike the enemy of God and Man, a type and representative of all things evil, we need not wonder when he fell by an arrow in the New Forest, that men saw a visible judgment of God.

To him, and to Henry the First, are commonly ascribed the ferocity of the Forest Laws. Men believed that in after time kings would have

* Constitutional History of England, I. Ed., Vol. I., p. 289.

mitigated matters had it been in their power. They said, and there is much truth in the averment, that these bad laws required the support of an army of evil men to work them efficiently, and that for the ordinary court officials, or the king himself, to thwart these people would be especially dangerous. When we call to mind what have been from time to time the characters of the farmers of the taxes at Naples, and various parts of France, we cannot deny that there is much truth in the statement.

Affairs reached their most evil point when Henry II. was King. It was then the custom for the royal foresters to be a complete law unto themselves, they put to death and mutilated whom they would without any trial whatever, or with but the mockery of the water-ordeal, a farce which had already been condemned by the Church, but which was very fashionable with ruffians who were anxious to secure a conviction. One of these fellows laid hold of an ecclesiastic, with the intention of extracting from him a large sum of money. Well was it for him that he was of the diocese of Lincoln, and that at that time Hugh of Avalon was its bishop. The thunders of excommunication were at once heard, the ecclesiastic escaped from the forester's clutches, and from that time forward, though much yet remained to be done, the tide turned, and the Forest Laws were administered with something more nearly approaching to justice.

Trial by Jury in Old Times.

By Thomas Frost.

WHEN we congratulate ourselves, as we are so apt to do, on the length of time the system of trial by jury has been established in England, and the safeguard it affords against attempts to strain the law to the prejudice of the accused, we are often unmindful of the fact that the institution has not always proved a safeguard when the court, acting under the influence of the Crown, endeavoured to obtain a conviction. It was only in the latter half of the sixteenth century that juries began to evince that determination not to yield their own judgment to the wishes of those in high authority, which became further developed in the course of the seventeenth. An interesting illustration of the old spirit of judges, and the new spirit of juries, is afforded by the trial of Sir Nicholas Throckmorton, in 1554, on a charge of high treason, in conspiring the death or deposition of the Queen, and the seizure by force of arms of the Tower of London. The prosecution was conducted by Serjeant Stanford and the Attorney-General, Griffin, the former leading; and it is noteworthy that both they and Chief Justice Bromley questioned the prisoner in much the same manner as is still customary in France and Belgium, striving to procure evidence that would convict him out of his own mouth. The endeavour failed, and the only criminating evidence against the prisoner was contained in the alleged confessions of Winter and Crofts, who, however, were not called as witnesses.

The jury, after several hours' deliberation, returned a verdict of not guilty, upon which the Lord Chief Justice addressed them in threatening tones, saying, "Remember yourselves better. Have you considered substantially the whole evidence as it was declared and recited? The matter doth touch the Queen's highness and yourselves also. Take good heed what you do." The jury were firm, however, and the foreman replied to the remonstrance of the bench, "We have found him not guilty, agreeable to all our consciences." Then the Attorney-General rose, and addressing the court, said, "An it please you, my lords, forasmuch as it seemeth these men of the jury, which have strangely acquitted the prisoner of his treasons whereof he was indicted, will forthwith depart the court, I pray you for the Queen that they and every one of them may be bound in a recognizance of £500 a-piece, to answer to such matters as they shall be charged with in the Queen's behalf, whensoever they shall be charged or called." The court went beyond even this audacious request, for they actually committed the jury to prison! Four of them were discharged shortly afterwards, having so little moral stamina left as to make a humble confession that they had done wrong; but the remaining eight were brought before the Star Chamber and severely dealt with, three being ordered to pay a fine of £2,000 each, and the others £200 each.

In the following reign, in a case in which three persons were indicted for murder, and the jury found them guilty of manslaughter only, contrary to the direction of the court, the jurors were both fined and bound in recognizances for their future "good behaviour." A decision of the Lord Chancellor, the two Chief Justices, and the Chief Baron, in the reign of James I., sets forth that when a person is found *guilty* on indictment, the jury should not be questioned; but when a jury has acquitted a prisoner against what the court holds to be proof of guilt, they may be charged in the Star Chamber, "for their partiality in finding a manifest offender not guilty." In 1667, we find this view extended to the case of grand juries ignoring a bill on grounds which the court did not consider sufficient, Chief Justice Kelying in that year having fined a grand jury of the County of Somerset, for not finding a true bill against a man accused of murder; but, says the report, "because they were gentlemen of repute in the county, the court spared the fine." This case, and several others in which the same judge had acted in a similar manner, were brought under the notice of the House of Commons, however, and that assembly resolved "that the precedents and practice of fining or imprisoning jurors for verdicts is illegal."

Notwithstanding this resolution of the House of Commons, William Penn, and another member of the Society of Friends, named Mead, being indicted at the Old Bailey for having, with other persons unknown, unlawfully and tumultuously assembled in Gracechurch Street, in the City of London, the Recorder dealt with the jury in a manner which caused the illegality of fining jurors for their verdicts to be again brought into question. The indictment set forth that Penn, by agreement with and abetment of Mead, did in the open street speak and preach to the persons there assembled, by reason whereof a great concourse of people gathered and remained a long time, in contempt of the King and the law, and to the great terror and disturbance of many of His Majesty's liege subjects. The trial took place before the Recorder, the Lord Mayor, and the Aldermen ; and when witnesses had deposed that Penn had preached, and that Mead was there with him, the Recorder summed up the evidence, and the jury retired to consider their verdict. They were absent a considerable time, at length returning with the verdict that Penn was " guilty of speaking in Gracechurch Street."

" Is that all ? " the Recorder asked.

" That is all I have in commission," replied the foreman.

"You had as good say nothing," observed the Recorder, and the Lord Mayor added, " Was it not an unlawful assembly ? You mean he was speaking to a tumult of people there."

" My lord," returned the foreman, " that is all I have in commission."

" The law of England," said the Recorder " will

not allow you to part until you have given in your verdict."

"We have given in our verdict," returned the jury, "and we can give in no other."

"Gentlemen," said the Recorder, "you have not given in your verdict, and you had as good say nothing; therefore go and consider it once more, that we may make an end of this troublesome business."

The jury then asked for pen, ink, and paper, and the request being complied with, they again retired, returning after a brief interval with their verdict in writing. They found Penn "guilty of speaking or preaching to an assembly met together in Gracechurch Street," and Mead not guilty.

"Gentlemen," said the Recorder, regarding the jury angrily, "you shall not be dismissed till we have a verdict that the court will accept; and you shall be locked up, without meat, drink, fire, and tobacco. You shall not think thus to abuse the court. We will have a verdict, or you shall starve for it."

Penn protested against this course, upon which the Recorder ordered the officers of the court to stop his mouth or remove him. The jury not leaving their box, the Recorder again directed them to retire and re-consider their verdict. Penn made a spirited remonstrance. "The agreement of twelve men," said he, "is a verdict in law, and such a one having been given by the jury, I require the clerk of the peace to record it, as he will answer at his peril. And if the jury bring in another verdict contradictory to this, I affirm they are perjured men in law. You are Englishmen," he added, turning to the jury, "mind your privilege; give not away your right." The court then adjourned to the following morning, when the prisoners were brought to the bar, and the jury, who had been locked up all night, were sent for. They were firm of purpose, and through their foreman persisted in their verdict.

"What is this to the purpose?" demanded the Recorder, "I will have a verdict." Then addressing a juror, named Bushel, whom he had threatened on the previous day, he said, "you are a factious fellow; I will set a mark on you, and whilst I have anything to do in the city, I will have an eye on you."

Penn again protested against the jury being threatened in this manner, upon which the Lord Mayor ordered that his mouth should be stopped, and that the gaoler should bring fetters and chain him to the floor; but it does not appear that this was done. The jury were again directed to retire and bring in a different verdict, and they withdrew under protest, the foreman saying, "We have given in our verdict, and all agreed to it; and if we give in another, it will be a force upon us to save our lives."

According to the narrative written by Penn and Mead, and quoted in Forsyth's "History of Trial by Jury," this scene took place on Sunday morning, and the court adjourned again to the following day, when, unless they were supplied with food surreptitiously, they must have fasted since Saturday. The foreman gave in their verdict in writing, as before, to which they had severally subscribed their names. The clerk received it, but was prevented from reading it by the Recorder, who desired him to ask for a "positive verdict."

"That is our verdict," said the foreman. "We have subscribed to it."

"Then hearken to your verdict," said the clerk. "You say that William Penn is not guilty in manner and form as he stands indicted; you say that William Mead is not guilty in manner and form as he stands indicted ; and so say you all."

The jury responded affirmatively, and their names were then called over, and each juror was commanded to give his separate verdict, which they did unanimously.

"I am sorry, gentlemen," the Recorder then said, "you have followed your own judgments and opinions, rather than the good and wholesome advice which was given you. God keep my life out of your hands! But for this the court fines you forty marks a man, and imprisonment till paid."

Penn was about to leave the dock, but was prevented from doing so, upon which he said, "I demand my liberty, being freed by the jury."

"You are in for your fines," the Lord Mayor told the prisoners.

"Fines, for what?" demanded Penn.

"For contempt of court," replied the Lord Mayor.

"I ask," exclaimed Penn, "if it be according to the fundamental laws of England, that any Englishman should be fined or amerced but by the judgment of his peers or jury; since it expressly contradicts the fourteenth and twenty-ninth chapters of the Great Charter of England, which say, 'No freeman ought to be amerced but by the oath of good and lawful men of the vicinage.'"

"Take him away," cried the Recorder.

"They then," continues the narrative, "hauled the prisoners into the bail-dock, and from thence sent them to Newgate, for non-payment of their fines ; and so were their jury. But the jury were afterwards discharged upon an *habeas corpus*, returnable in the Common Pleas, where their commitment was adjudged illegal." Even then, judges appear to have remained unconvinced of the illegality of the practice, or stubborn in their desire to enforce their own views or wishes upon juries ; for the question was not regarded as finally settled until the decision in the Court of Common Pleas was clinched, in the same year, by a similar judgment of the Court of King's Bench.

Barbarous Punishments.

By Sidney W. Clarke.

THAT the world has become more merciful as it has grown older, is a truism at once apparent to anyone who gives even a cursory glance at any of the numerous works dealing with the criminal laws of the olden time. Still the approach to the most excellent quality has been regretably and painfully slow, and it is surely a stain on the boasted enlightenment of the nineteenth century, that the century had run through nearly three-fourths of its existence before the terrible and vindictive punishment of drawing and quartering disappeared from our statute book. In most States the early laws have been of a blood-thirsty and fear-inspiring nature, but what excuse can be urged for the fact that until the fourth day of July, in the year of Grace 1870, the punishment ordained by law for the crime of high treason, was that the unfortunate offender should be drawn on a hurdle to the place of execution, there to be hanged by the neck till he be dead; that his head be severed from his body; that his body be divided into four quarters; and that his head and quarters be at the disposal of the Crown. In Blackstone's time the sentence was still more savage, or, as the great Commentator puts it, "very solemn and terrible." It was that the offender be drawn to the gallows, and not be carried or walk; "though usually," says Blackstone, "by connivance, at length ripened by humanity into law, a sledge or hurdle was allowed to preserve the offender from the extreme torment of being dragged on the ground or pavement;" that he be hanged by the neck and then cut down alive; that his entrails be taken out, and burned before his eyes, while he was still alive; that his head be cut off, his body be divided into four parts, and his head and quarters be at the King's disposal. What our tender-hearted monarchs did with the quivering pieces of flesh let the stones of Temple Bar, the City Gates, and the Tower bear witness. Here are a couple of extracts from that perennial fountain of information, the diary of Mr. Samuel Pepys. Under date of October 13th, 1660, he writes, "I went out to Charing Cross to see Major-

General Harrison," one of the regicides, "hanged, drawn, and quartered, which was done there, *he looking as cheerful as any man could do in that condition.*" Note the grim humour of the words in italics. "He was presently cut down, and his head and heart shown to the people, at which there was great shouts of joy." Again, on October 20th, in the same year:—"This afternoon going through London and calling at Crowe's, the upholsterer's, in St. Bartholomew's, I saw the limbs of some of our new traytors set upon Aldersgate, which was a sad sight to see; and a bloody week this and the last have been, there being ten hanged, drawn, and quartered."

It will be observed that the masculine gender is used in the foregoing sentences for high treason; for, if the offender was a woman, the law with a delicacy (!) one would hardly have expected, recognised that "the decency due to the sex forbids the exposing and publicly mutilating their bodies;" so a woman was simply to be drawn to the gallows, and there burned alive. And these punishments for treason Sir Edward Coke attempted to justify on Scriptural grounds, adding "it is punishment undoubtedly just, for our liege lord the King is lord of every one of our members, and they have severally conspired against him, and should each one suffer." Evidently justice has not always spelt humanity.

Another of the horrible punishments decreed by English law was that of boiling to death, which in the reign of Henry VIII. was inflicted for poisoning, and recalls the most cruel tortures of China and the Orient, where slicing to death and impalement alive are or were common forms of punishment. The awful fate of being boiled alive was specially devised for the benefit of John Roose, a cook, who had been convicted of throwing poison into a pot of broth intended for the family of the Bishop of Rochester and for the poor of the Parish; in 1542, Margaret Davey suffered the same lingering death at Smithfield. So fearful were our ancestors of poison, that in Scotland, in 1601, Thomas Bellie, a burgess of Brechin, and his son were banished for life by the High Court of Justiciary, for the heinous offence of poisoning a couple of troublesome hens belonging to a neighbour. Even the laws of Draco, said on account of their severity to have been written not in ink but in blood, can scarcely compete with these examples of British barbarity.

Among the Romans strangulation, precipitation from a rocky height (a mode of carrying out the death sentence still found amongst savage tribes), and lashing to death were forms of punishment. Soldiers guilty of military offences had to run the gauntlet. Upon a given signal all the soldiers of the legion to which the offender belonged fell upon him with sticks and stones, and generally killed him on the spot. If, however, he succeeded in making his escape, he was thenceforth an exile from his native country. Offending slaves were first scourged and then crucified. They were compelled to carry the cross to the place of execution, and after being suspended were left to perish by slow degrees. Crucifixion was abolished throughout the Roman Empire by Constantine, out of reverence to the sacred symbol. Other cruel punishments were burning alive, exposure to wild animals, and condemnation to fight as gladiators in the arena for the amusement of the citizens. The second of these modes of death, for death was the invariable result, was the one usually meted out to the early Christians—" If the Tiber overflows its banks; if there be a famine or plague; if there be a cold, a dry, or a scorching season; if any public calamity overtakes us; the universal cry of the people is—" To the lion with the Christians—*Christiani ad leonem!*"

Parricide was punished in a strange manner. The criminal, after being scourged, was tied or sewed up in a leather bag, with a dog, a cock, a viper, and an ape to keep him company, and so cast into the sea. The Egyptians punished the same offence by sticking the prisoner all over with pointed reeds, and then throwing him upon a fire of burning thorns, where he lay till he was consumed.

With most nations the *Lex talionis*, or punishment of retaliation—an eye for an eye, a limb for a limb—has found a place in the penal system. It was not, indeed, always carried out to its logical conclusion, but rather became the subject of many subtle distinctions. Among the Athenians, Solon decreed that whoever put out the eye of a one-eyed person should for so doing lose both his own. But what, it was asked, should be done where a one-eyed man happened to put out one of his neighbour's eyes? Should he lose his only eye by way of retaliation? If so, he would then be quite blind, and would so suffer a greater injury than he had caused. The law of the Jews and Egyptians compelled anyone, who without lawful excuse was found with a deadly poison in his possession, to himself swallow the poison. An instance of a kind of *lex talionis* in our own country is found in the reign of Edward I., when incendiaries were burnt to death. Another example is that, from the reign of Henry VIII. to that of George IV., to strike a blow and draw blood within the precincts of the King's palace, entailed on the offender the loss of his right hand. Here are some of the regulations prescribed by the statute 33 Henry VIII., chapter 12, for the infliction of the punishment :—

> "viii. And for the further declaration of the solemn and due circumstance of the execution appertaining and of long time used and accustomed, to and for such malicious strikings, by reason whereof blood is, hath been, or hereafter shall be shed against the King's peace. It is therefore enacted by the authority aforesaid, that the Sergeant or Chief Surgeon for the time being, or his deputy of the King's household, his heirs and successors, shall be ready at the time and place of execution, as shall be appointed as is aforesaid, to sear the stump when the hand is stricken off.
>
> "ix. And the Sergeant of the Pantry shall be also then and there ready to give bread to the party that shall have his hand so stricken off.
>
> "x. And the Sergeant of the Cellar shall also be then and there ready with a pot of red wine to give the

same party drink after his hand is so stricken off and the stump seared.

"xi. And the Sergeant of the Ewry shall also be then and there ready with cloths sufficient for the Surgeon to occupy about the same execution.

"xii. And the Yeoman of the Chandry shall also be then and there, and have in readiness seared cloths sufficient for the Surgeon to occupy about the same execution.

"xiii. And the Master Cook shall be also then and there ready, and shall bring with him a dressing-knife, and shall deliver the same knife at the place of execution to the Sergeant of the Larder, who shall be also then and there ready, and hold upright the dressing-knife till execution be done."

" xiv. And the Sergeant of the Poultry shall be also then and there ready with a cock in his hand, ready for the Surgeon to wrap about the same stump, when the hand shall be so stricken off.

"xv. And the Yeoman of the Scullery to be also then and there ready, and prepare and make at the place of execution a fire of coals, and there to make ready searing-irons against the said Surgeon or his deputy shall occupy the same.

"xvi. And the Sergeant or Chief Ferror shall be also then and there ready, and bring with him the searing-irons, and deliver the same to the same Sergeant or Chief Surgeon or to his deputy when they be hot.

"xvii. And the Groom of the Salcery shall be also then and there ready with vinegar and cold water, and give attendance upon the said Surgeon or his deputy until the same execution be done.

"xviii. And the Sergeant of the Woodyard shall bring to the said place of execution a block, with a betil, a staple, and cords to bind the said hand upon the block while execution is in doing."

In addition to losing his hand, the unfortunate offender was imprisoned for life. It was not until 1829 that this punishment was abolished, after having been in existence for a period of 287 years.

A curious mode of punishment, intended to make its victim the object of popular ridicule, was in vogue in the ancient German Empire, where persons who endeavoured to create tumults and to disturb the public tranquility were condemned to carry a dog upon their shoulders from one large town to another.

The penal laws of France were every wit as inhuman as our own—burning alive, breaking on the wheel, hanging, beheading, and quartering were common forms of punishment. Awful atrocities were committed on living victims, such as tearing off the flesh with red-hot pincers, pouring molten lead and brimstone into the wounds, and cutting out the tongue. The following is the sentence passed upon Ravaillac, the assassin of Henry IV., in 1610 :—He was first to be privily tortured and then carried to the place of execution. There the flesh was to be torn with red-hot pincers from his breasts, his arms and thighs, and the calves of his legs; his right hand, holding the knife wherewith he committed his crime, was to be scorched and burned with flaming brimstone; on the places where the flesh had been torn off a mixture of melted lead, boiling oil, scalding pitch, wax, and brimstone was to be poured; after this he was to be torn in pieces by four horses, and his limbs and body burned to ashes and dispersed in the air. His goods and chattels were confiscated; the house in which he was born was pulled down; his father and mother were banished, and his other relatives commanded to change the name of Ravaillac for some other. This sentence was not, surely, a vindication of outraged justice, but rather a purile and barbarous legal revenge.

To return to the laws of our own country. Multilation of one sort or another was long a favourite mode of punishment; pulling out the tongue for slander, cutting off the nose for adultery, emasculation for counterfeiting money, and so on. In Foxe's "Book of Martyrs" there is an account of a miracle which was worked on the person of a mutilated criminal. A Bedfordshire man was convicted of theft, and for his crime his eyes were pulled out and other abominable mutilations were inflicted on him. The sufferer repaired to the shrine of St. Thomas at Canterbury, where after devout and steadfast prayer the parts he had lost were, so we are told, miraculously restored. Anyone who fought with weapons in a church had an ear cut off, or if he had already lost both his ears was branded in the cheek with the letter F.

By an Act passed in the reign of Queen Elizabeth, the punishment for forgery was that the offender should stand in the pillory and have his ears cut off by the common hangman, his nostrils slit up and seared, and then suffer imprisonment for life. In 1731 Joseph Cook, aged 70 years, underwent this punishment, the mutilation taking place while he stood in the pillory at Charing Cross.

The Coventry Act (22-23 Charles II., chapter 1.) was passed in consequence of Sir John Coventry having been assaulted in the street and his nose slit, out of revenge as was supposed. It enacted that if any person should of malice, aforethought, and by lying in wait, cut out or disable the tongue, put out an eye, slit the nose, or cut off or disable any limb or member of any other person, with intent to maim or to disfigure him, such person, his councillors, aiders, and abettors, should be guilty of felony without benefit of clergy, which implied the punishment of death. This Act was not repealed until 1828, and resulted in at least one curious case. In 1772, one Coke and a labourer named Woodburn were indicted under the Act—Coke for hiring and abetting Woodburn, and Woodburn for the actual offence of slitting the nose of one Crispe, who was Coke's brother-in-law. The intention of the accused was to murder Crispe, and they left him for dead, having terribly hacked and disfigured him with a hedge-bill, but he recovered. An attempt to murder was not then a felony, but under the Coventry Act to disfigure with an intent to disfigure was; and the accused were indicted for the latter offence. Coke, in the course of his defence, raised the point that the attack on Crispe was made with intent to murder him and not with intent to disfigure, therefore, he contended, the offence was not within the statute under which he was indicted. But the court held that if a man attacked another intending to murder him, with such an instrument as a hedge-bill, which could not but endanger a disfiguring of the victim, and in such attack happened not to kill but only to disfigure, he might be indicted for disfiguring. The jury found the prisoners guilty, and they were condemned and duly executed.

The laws for the protection of trade decreed many cruel punishments. Thus, in the reign of Elizabeth, an Act passed for the encouragement of the woollen industry prescribed that the penalty for taking live sheep out of the country should be forfeiture of goods, imprisonment for a year, and that at the end of the year the left hand of the prisoner should be cut off in a public market, and be there nailed up in the most public place. A second offence was punishable with death. By statute 21 James 1, chapter 19, anyone unfortunate enough to become a bankrupt was nailed by one ear to the pillory for two hours, and then had the ear cut off. Under the Romans a bankrupt was treated still more unmercifully, for at the option of his creditors he was either cut to pieces or sold to foreigners beyond the Tiber.

A longstanding disgrace to the intelligence and humanity of our countrymen was the fact that in former times burning alive was the inevitable fate of poor wretches convicted of witchcraft, the penal laws against which were not repeated until 1736.

BARBAROUS PUNISHMENTS. 145

So late as 1712, five so called witches were hung at Northampton, and in 1716 Mrs Hicks, and her daughter, aged nine, were condemned to death at Huntingdon for selling their souls to the devil. Even children of tender years were not spared, but with their elders alike fell victims to our law's barbarity; there are many recorded instances of children under ten years of age being executed. In Scotland the last execution for witchcraft took place in 1722.

Space will not permit any attempt to run through the whole gamut of legal iniquities; at most we can only attempt a very incomplete catalogue of the inhumanities at one time or another incident to our penal codes, and with a final horror we must bring this article to an end. The punishment with which we are now about to deal, that of pressing to death, *peine forte et dure* as it was called, is perhaps the most noteable example of the former barbarity of our law, since it was inflicted before trial on innocent and guilty alike, who refused to plead "Guilty" or "Not Guilty" to an indictment for felony. What this punishment was, which was first instituted in 1406, can best be told by giving the form of the judgment of the court against the person who refused to plead :—That the prisoner shall be remanded to the place from whence he came, and put in some low, dark room, and that he shall lie without any litter or other thing under him, and without any manner of covering; that one arm shall be drawn to one quarter of the room with a cord and the other to another, and that his feet shall be used in the same manner; and that as many weights shall be laid upon him as he can bear, and more; that he shall have three morsels of barley bread a day, and that he shall have the water next the prison, so that it be not current; and that he shall not eat the same day on which he drinks, nor drink the same day on which he eats; and that he shall continue so till he die or answer.

Peine forte et dure was not abolished till 1772, and was frequently undergone by accused persons in order to preserve their estates from being forfeited to the Crown, which would have been the case if they had stood their trial and been found guilty. The year 1741 is probably the last date on which the punishment was inflicted. In 1721, two men, Thomas Cross and Thomas Spigot, were ordered to be pressed to death at the Old Bailey. Cross gave in on seeing the preparations made for his torture, but Spigot was made of sterner stuff. In the "Annals of Newgate" is a description of his sufferings:—"The chaplain found him lying in the vault upon the bare ground with 350 pounds weight upon his breast, and then prayed by him, and at several times asked him why he would hazard his soul by such obstinate kind of self-murder. But all the answer that he made was—'Pray for me, pray for me!' He sometimes lay silent under the pressure, as if insensible to pain, and then again would fetch his breath very quick and short. Several times he complained that they had laid a cruel weight upon his face, though it was covered with nothing but a thin cloth, which was afterwards removed and laid more light and hollow; yet he still complained of the prodigious weight upon his face, which might be caused by the blood being forced up thither, and pressing the veins as violently as if the force had been externally upon his face. When he had remained for half-an-hour under this load, and 50 pounds weight more laid on, being in all 400 pounds, he told those who attended him he would plead. The weights were at once taken off, the cords cut asunder; he was raised by two men, some brandy was put into his mouth to revive him, and he was carried to take his trial." In 1735, a man, who pretended to be dumb at the Sussex Assizes, was sent to Horsham Gaol to be pressed to death unless he would plead. He endured in agony a weight of 350 pounds, and then the executioner, who weighed over 16 stones, laid himself upon the board upon which the weights were placed, and killed the wretched man instantly.

Trials of Animals.

By Thomas Frost.

ONE of the most singular features of the jurisprudence of the middle ages, and one which was retained in the French code down to nearly the middle of the last century, was the indictment of domestic animals for injuries inflicted on mankind. The records of the criminal tribunals of France disclose ninety-two such judicial processes between 1120 and 1741, when the last of these grotesque trials took place in Poitou. The practice seems to have been based on the Mosaic law, it being there ordered that, "if an ox gore a man or a woman that they die, then the ox shall be stoned, and his flesh shall not be eaten." (Exodus, c. xxi., v. 28.) Oxen and pigs were the animals that most frequently were the subjects of these strange proceedings, the indictment against the former being for goring persons, while the latter suffered for killing and sometimes devouring very young children.

The earliest instance of which any particulars

can be gathered occurred in 1314, when, according to M. Carlier, who relates the story in his history of the Duchy of Valois, a bull escaped from a farm-yard in the village of Moisy, and gored a man so severely that death ensued. The Count of Valois, being informed of the fatility, directed that the bull should be captured, and formally prosecuted for causing the man's death. This was done, and evidence was given by persons who had seen the man attacked and killed. The bull was thereupon sentenced to suffer death, which was inflicted by strangulation, after which the carcase was suspended from a tree by the hind legs. But the affair did not end thus, for the sentence was appealed against, probably by the owner of the bull, on the ground that the retainers of the Count of Valois had no legal authority to execute the sentence. This plea was debated at great length, and the provincial parliament eventually decided that, though the sentence was a just one, the Count of Valois had no justiciary authority in the district of Moisy.

Next in the order of time comes the trial at Falaise of a sow which had torn the face and arm of a child, from the effects of which injuries it died. The sow was condemned to be mutilated

TRIALS OF ANIMALS. 151

in the head and one fore leg, and afterwards to be strangled, which sentence was executed in the public square of the town. This was in 1386. Three years later, a horse was condemned to death at Dijon for having killed a man. In 1403, Simon de Baudemont, lieutenant of Meulan ; Jean, lord of Maintenon ; and the bailiff of Mantes and Meulan, signed an attestation of the expenses incurred in the prosecution and execution of a sow that had killed and partially eaten a child. The following is a copy of the document, to which it may be added that the story of the trial and execution may be found in the "Curiosités Judiciaires et Historiques du Moyen Age" of M. Aguel :—" Item, for expenses within the gaol, 6 sols. Item, to the executioner, who came from Paris to Meulan to put the sentence in execution, by command of our Lord the Bailiff and of the King's Attorney, 54 sols. Item, for the carriage that conveyed her to execution, 6 sols. Item, for ropes to tie and haul her up, 2 sols, 8 deniers. Item, for gloves, 12 deniers ; amounting in the whole to 69 sols, 8 deniers." In connection with the first item of this curious document, it may be observed that, in a receipt delivered five years later by a notary of Pont de l'Arche to the gaoler of the prison of that town, the same amount is allowed for the daily food of a pig, imprisoned on the charge of killing a child, as for a man in the same prison. The last item, the gloves, is supposed by M. Aguel to be a customary allowance to the executioner.

In 1457, a sow and her six young pigs were tried at Lavegny, on the charge of having killed and partially eaten a child. The sow was convicted, and condemned to death; but the little ones were acquitted on the ground of their tender years or months, the bad example of their mother, and the absence of direct evidence of their having partaken of the unnatural feast. In 1494, sentence of death was pronounced on a pig by the Mayor of Laon for having mutilated and destroyed an infant in its cradle, full particulars of which case were given in the "Annuaire du Departement de l'Aisne" for 1812. The act of condemnation, as there given, concludes as follows:—"We, in detestation and horror of this crime, and in order to make an example and satisfy justice, have declared, judged, sentenced, pronounced, and appointed that the said hog, being detained a prisoner, and confined in the said abbey, shall be, by the executioner, strangled and hanged on a gibbet, near and adjoining the gallows in the jurisdiction of the said monks, being near their copyhold of Avin. In witness of which we have sealed this present with our seal." This document was sealed with red wax, and endorsed :—" Sentence on a hog, executed by justice, brought into the copyhold of Clermont, and strangled on a gibbet at Avin."

Three years later, a sow was condemned to be beaten to death for having mutilated the face of a child of the village of Charonne. The act of condemnation in this case directed further that the flesh of the sow should be given to the dogs of the village, and that the owner of the sow and his wife should make a pilgrimage to the Church of Our Lady at Pontoise, and bring on their return a certificate that this injunction had been duly complied with. In 1499, a bull was strangled for having killed a boy in the lordship of Cauroy, which belonged to the abbey of Beaufiré.

Lionnois gives, in his history of Nancy, a full report of the proceedings on the delivery of a condemned pig to the executioner of that city in 1572. He mentions, among other details, that the animal, secured by a cord, was led to a cross near the cemetery; that from the most remote period the justice of the lord, the abbot of Moyen Moutier, was accustomed to deliver to the provost, or marshal of St. Diez, near to this cross, all condemned criminals, that execution might ensue; and that, the said pig being a brute beast, the mayor and the justice held a conference at that place, and left the said pig tied with a cord, without prejudice to the judicial rights of the lord.

Judicial proceedings against the lower animals were not confined to France, for the list of such cases compiled by M. Berriat St. Prix, and published in the "Memoires de la Societé des Antiquaires" for 1829, mentions one tried at Lausanne in 1364, another at the same town in 1451, a third at Basle in 1474, another at Lausanne in 1479, and a fifth at the same place in 1554. Concerning the first of these Swiss trials, Ruchat states, in his history of the Protestant reformation in Switzerland, that the victim was a pig that had killed a child in the village of Chattens, situated among the Jorat hills. It was cited to appear in the Bishop's Court at Lausanne, convicted of murder, and sentenced to death—the executioner being a pork butcher.

The Basle case was a very singular one. A farm-yard cock was tried on the absurd charge of having laid an egg. It was contended in support of the prosecution that eggs laid by cocks were of inestimable value for use in certain magical preparations; that a sorcerer would rather possess a cock's egg than the philosopher's stone; and that Satan employed witches to hatch such eggs, from which proceeded winged serpents most dangerous to mankind. On behalf of the gallinaceous prisoner, the facts of the case were admitted, but his advocate submitted that no evil animus had been proved against his client, and that no injury to man or beast had resulted. Besides, the laying of the egg was an involuntary act, and as such not punishable by law. If it was intended to impute the crime of sorcery to his client, he was entitled to an acquittal; for there was no instance on record of Satan having made a compact with one of the brute creation. In reply, the public prosecutor stated that, though the Evil One did not make compacts with brutes, he sometimes entered into them; and though the swine possessed by devils, as related by the Evangelists, were involuntary agents, yet they, nevertheless, were punished by being caused to run down a steep decline into the Lake of Galilee, where they were drowned. The poor cock was convicted, and condemned to death, not as a cock, however, but as a sorcerer, or perhaps a devil, in the form of a cock, on which finding it was, with the egg attributed to it, burned at a stake, with all the form and solemnity of a judicial execution.

As the lower animals were amenable to the law in Switzerland in those dark ages, so, in certain circumstances, they could be put into the witness box. If a house was broken into between sunset and sunrise, and the occupier killed the intruder, the act was regarded as justifiable homicide. But it was thought right to provide by law against the case of a man, living alone, who might invite a person whom he wished to kill to spend the evening with him, and having slain him, might assert that he committed the act in self-defence, or to protect his property, the dead man having been a burglar. Therefore, when a man was killed in such circumstances, the occupier of the house was required to produce some domestic animal that was an inmate of the house, and had witnessed the tragedy, and to declare his innocence on oath in the presence of such animal. If the brute witness did not contradict him, he was acquitted ; the law taking it for granted that God, rather than allow a murderer to go unpunished, would intervene by causing a miraculous manifestation by the mouth of a dumb witness.

Even more strange than the trials of oxen, pigs, etc., for offences against mankind, were the legal proceedings often taken in the middle ages against noxious insects and the smaller quadrupeds, such as rats. The "Memoires de la Societé Royale Academique de Savoie" contain a very curious account of the proceedings instituted in 1445 and 1487 against certain beetles that had committed great ravages in the vineyards of St. Julien. Advocates were named on behalf of the vine-growers and the beetles respectively; but, by a singular coincidence, the insects disappeared when cited to answer for the mischief they had done, and the proceedings were in consequence abandoned. That was in 1445. In 1487, however, they re-appeared, and a complaint was thereupon addressed to the vicar-general of the Bishop of Maurienne, who named a judge, and also an advocate to represent the beetles. Counsel having been heard on both sides, the judge suggested that the vine-growers should cede to the defendants certain land, where they could live without encroaching on the vineyards. The plaintiffs agreed to this compromise, with the proviso that, in default of the defendants accepting the terms offered them, the judge would order that the vineyards should be respected by the beetles under certain penalties. The advocate for the beetles demanded time for consideration, and on the resumption of the proceedings stated that he could not accept, on behalf of his clients, the suggestion of the court, as the land proposed to be given up to them was barren, and afforded nothing upon which they could subsist. The court then appointed assessors to survey the land in question, and on their report that it was well wooded and provided with herbage, the conveyance was ordered to be engrossed in due form and executed. The matter was then regarded by the plaintiffs as settled; but the beetles discovered, or their advocate discovered for them, that a quarry of an ochreous earth, used as a pigment, had formerly been worked on the land conveyed to the insects, and though it had long since been worked out, some person possessed an ancient right of way to it, the exercise of which would be extremely prejudicial to them. Consequently, the agreement was held to be vitiated, and the legal proceedings had to be recommenced *de novo*. How they eventually terminated cannot be told, owing to the mutilation of the documents relating to the proceedings subsequent to 1487.

Nearly a century later, legal proceedings were commenced by the inhabitants of a village in the diocese of Autun against the rats by which their houses and barns were infested; the trial being famous in the annals of French jurisprudence as that in which Chassanee, the celebrated jurisconsult, first achieved distinction. The rats not appearing on the first citation, Chassanee, who was retained for the defence, argued that the summons was of too local a character, and that, as all the rats in the diocese of Autun were interested in the case, they should be summoned throughout the diocese. This plea being admitted, the curé of every parish in the diocese was instructed to summon all the rats within its limits to attend on a day named in the summons. The day having arrived, and the rats failing to appear, Chassanee said that, as all his clients were summoned, including old and young, sick and healthy, great preparations had to be made, and certain necessary arrangements effected, and he had to ask, therefore, for an extension of time. This also being granted, another day was appointed, but again not a single rat put in an appearance.

Chassanee then made an objection to the legality of the summons. A summons from that court, he said, implied full protection to the parties summoned, both on their way to it and on their return to their homes; and his clients, the rats, though most anxious to appear in obedience to the court, did not dare to leave their homes to come to Autun, on account of the number of evil-disposed cats kept by the plaintiffs. If the latter would enter into bonds, under heavy pecuniary penalties, that their cats should not molest his clients, the summons would be immediately obeyed. The court acknowledged the validity of this plea, but the plaintiffs declined to be bound for the good behaviour of their cats. The further hearing of the case was, therefore, adjourned *sine die*, and thus Chassanee gained his cause. Full particulars of the proceedings are given in a Latin work, written by him, and published in 1588.

Devices of the Sixteenth Century Debtors.

By James C. Macdonald, f.s.a., Scot.

IN the year 1531, a certain John Scott, residenter in the good town of Edinburgh, was financially in a condition of chronic decrepitude. His household goods were rapidly going to the hammer, and one creditor, bolder than his fellows, decided to attack the impecunious personality of the common debtor. Writs from court and messengers of the law were severally set in motion; and on the earliest possible day one of those myrmidons served upon the debtor personally, a writ bearing the terrible title of "Letters of IV Forms." The "coinless" John was therein warned that if he failed forthwith to pay or satisfy the lawful debt, for which decreet has gone out, he would (unless he went to prison in a peaceful way) be declared a rebel against the King's Majesty.

Now John reasoned with himself that payment he could not make; outlawry he rather feared;

and *squalor carceris* he could not endure. What was to be done? He had heard of the horns of of the Hebrew altars: how that personal safety resulted from any manual attachment thereto. Was there some such boon in bonny Scotland? There was Holyrood, with its sanctified abbey. It was near; any port in such a storm. Down the Canongate, and straight to the sanctuary he ran—all to the manifest loss, injury, and damage of his creditors who followed, having got wind of this unique *hegira* from the red-nosed city guard. In vain the creditors pleaded; equally in vain were their threats. The canny Scot was warranted safe and skaithless against "all mortal."

Annoyed at his debtor's immunity from arrest, chagrined that any money John possessed had now been further dissipated in the Abbey admission dues to its protection giving portals—each creditor turned sadly to his "buiks of Compts" and superscribed over against John Scott's name the expressive legend "bad debt." And this John Scott became the forerunner, *de facto*, of a long line of "distressed" persons. Nay more, he secured an immortality as lasting as that of the sovereign whose solemnly sounding

SIXTEENTH CENTURY DEBTORS. 163

"Letters of IV Forms," he spurned and left unanswered.

A generation later, and another *new* way of paying old debts is placed on record. To balance international honours it is of Anglican origin. Scoggan, the jester of the Elizabethan court, falls into financial distress. He borrows £500 from the Queen—*mirabile dictu*. Only a fool would have tried such a thing. It was put down as a "short loan," but it soon became clear to the royal lender that its longevity would outlast her reign. To all demands the clownish borrower smilingly cried "long live the queen," until at last his existence as court fool was in danger of being ended. But he would rather die than be evicted; and die he did. He became, theatrically speaking, defunct.

The *late* Scoggan was accordingly borne, to solemn music, past the royal garden; and the queen, seeing the mournful show—and knowing nought of its hollowness—asked whose it was. "Scoggan, Your Majesty," was the reply. "Poor fellow," she exclaimed, "the £500 he owed me I now freely forgive." Whereupon the "defunct" sat up and declared that the royal generosity had given him a new lease of life.

"Thou rogue," said the queen, "thou art more rogue than fool. Thou hast improved upon the plan of that John Scott, who, in the reign of my late cousin of Scotland, as Sir James Melvil tells me, got rid of the oldest debt and the longest loan."

Laws Relating to the Gipsies.

By William E. A. Axon, f.r.s.l.

EARLY in the fifteenth century the gipsies made their appearance in Europe, and as strangers were not favourably regarded in those days the advent of these dark-skinned people, speaking a language of their own, dressing in a picturesque, but uncommon costume, and having their own rulers, and their own code of morals, and owning no allegiance to the laws of the land in which they sojourned, naturally attracted attention. At first some credence was given to their high-sounding pretensions, and the dukes, counts, and lords of Lesser Egypt received safe conducts and protection under the idea that they were engaged in religious pilgrimages. But the seal of the Emperor Sigismund would not protect them when the term of their pretended pilgrimage had expired, nor would the manners and customs of the gipsies substantiate any special claim to sanctity or religious fervour. Even the ages when the divorce was most marked between religion and morals would be staggered by the thefts, and worse outrages that were laid to their charge. Sigismund's safe conducts are said to have been given not as Emperor, but as King of Hungary, and some of the gipsies were early employed as ironworkers in the realm of St. Stephen. In 1496 King Ladislaus gave a charter of protection to Thomas Polgar and his twenty five tents of gipsies because they had made musket bullets and other military stores for Bishop Sigismund at Fünfkirchen, but whatever consideration may have been shewn to them in the beginning, they speedily became objects of suspicion and dislike. There is not a country in Europe which has not legislated against them or endeavoured to exile them by administrative acts. Their expulsion from Spain was decreed in 1492, from France in 1562, and from various Italian states about the same time. Denmark, Sweden, and the Netherlands have also pronounced against them. The Diet of Augsburg in 1500, ordered their expulsion from Germany on the ground that they were spies of Turkey seeking to betray the Christians. This edict, though several times repeated, was non-effective.

In Hungary and Transylvania the authorities,

LAWS RELATING TO THE GIPSIES. 167

hopeless of getting rid of the troublesome immigrants, took strong measures to bring them into line with the rest of the population. They were prohibited from using the Romany tongue, from retaining their gipsy surnames, from wandering about the country, from eating carrion, and from dealing in horses. Those fit for military service were to be taken into the army, and the rest were to live and dress and deport themselves in the same manner as the peasantry of the country. These regulations were not wholly effective, but the result of the efforts put forward by Maria Theresa, and her successors may be seen in the sedentary gipsies of the Austro-Hungarian Empire. At times they have been subjected to fierce persecution. In 1782, a dreadful accusation was brought against the Hungarian Romanis, when more than a hundred of them were accused of murder and cannibalism. The gang were said to have lived by highway robbery and murder, and to have cooked and eaten the bodies of their victims. At Frauenmark four women were beheaded, six men were hanged, two were broken on the wheel, and one was quartered alive. Altogether forty-five were executed and many more were imprisoned.

How much of this was suspicion substantiated by torture?

The gipsies came frequently in contact with the myrmidons of the law. "As soon as the officer seizes or forces away the culprit," says Grellmann, " he is surrounded by a swarm of his comrades who take unspeakable pains to procure the release of the prisoner. . . . When it comes to the infliction of punishment, and the malefactor receives a good number of lashes well laid on, in the public market place, a universal lamentation commences among the vile crew; each stretches his throat to cry over the agony his dear associate is constrained to suffer. This is oftener the fate of the women than of the men; for as the maintenance of the family depends most upon them, they more frequently go out for plunder." It is a noteworthy fact that Grellmann writing in 1783, has not a word of condemnation of the barbarous practice of flogging women.

In England as elsewhere the earliest of these romantic people were welcomed. In 1519, the Earl of Surrey entertained "Gypsions" at Tendring Hall, Suffolk, and gave them a safe-conduct. Still earlier in 1505, Anthony Gaginus, Earl of Little Egypt, had a letter of recommen-

LAWS RELATING TO THE GIPSIES. 169

dation from James IV. of Scotland to the King of Denmark. James V. bestowed a charter upon James Faa, Lord and Earl of Little Egypt, by which he was privileged to execute justice upon his followers, much in the same way as the great barons were authorised to deal with their vassals. But they soon fell out of favour. In England, in the twenty-second year of Henry VIII. an act of parliament was passed which sets forth that there are certain outlandish people, who not profess any craft, or trade, whereby to maintain themselves, but go about in great numbers from place to place, using craft and subtlety to impose on people, making them believe that they understood the art of foretelling to men and women their good or ill fortune, by palmistry, whereby they frequently defraud people of their money, likewise are guilty of thefts and highway robberies; it is ordered that the said vagrants, commonly called Egyptians, in case they remain sixteen days in the kingdom, shall forfeit their goods and chattels to the king and be further liable to imprisonment. In 1537, Cromwell writes to the Lord President of the Marches of Wales, that the "Gipcyans" had promised to leave the kingdom in return for a general pardon for their previous offences, and exhorts the authorities to see that their deportation is effected. Many were sent to Norway, but the effort to extirpate them from the kingdom entirely failed.* By an act of 1554, a penalty of £40 was to be inflicted upon any one knowingly importing them. Those gipsies, following "their old accustomed devlishe and noughty practises," were to be treated as felons, but exception was made in favour of such as placed themselves in the service of some "honest and able inhabitant." Many were executed, but the remnant survived and managed to hold a yearly meeting at the Peak Cavern or Kelbrook, near Blackheath. Still sterner was the law passed in 1562-3, which made it felony for any one born within the kingdom to join the fellowship of vagabonds calling themselves Egyptians. The previous acts had referred to the gipsies as an outlandish people, but now the native born were brought equally within the meshes of this sanguinary law. "Throughout the reign of Elizabeth," as Borrow remarks, "there was a

---

* The Lord Chief Justice, John Popham, who was born in 1531, is said to have been stolen when a child by the gipsies. They disfigured him and placed on his arm a cabalistic mark. Apparently it was a case of tattooing. But the story is discredited.

terrible persecution of the gipsy race; far less, however, on account of the crimes which were actually committed, than from a suspicion which was entertained that they harboured amidst their companies priests and emissaries of Rome." The harrying of the missionary priests was in part dictated by the spirit of religious persecution, but in a still greater degree by the conviction that they were political emissaries, aiming at the subversion of the kingdom. The priests on the English mission had often to disguise themselves, and at times may have assumed the garb of wandering beggars, but they are not likely to have consorted with the Romans, whose language would be strange to them, and whose heathenish indifference to all dogmas, rites, and ceremonies, would be specially distasteful to zealous Catholics.

After "the spacious times" of great Elizabeth, the gipsies had a rest from special oppression, though they were of course still in jeopardy from the harsh laws as to vagrancy and those minor crimes, that are their characteristic failings. Romany girls were flogged for filching and fortune-telling, and Romany men were hanged for horse-stealing. They were looked upon with suspicion, and it was easy enough to raise prejudice against them. This was shewn in the notorious case of Elizabeth Canning. She was a girl of eighteen, employed as a domestic servant at Aldermanbury, and in 1753, disappeared for four weeks. On her return she asserted that she had been abducted and detained in a loft by gipsies, who gave her only bread and water to eat. Their aim she declared was to induce her to adopt an immoral life. Mrs. Wells, Mary Squires, George Squires, Virtue Hall, Fortune and Judith Natus, were arrested, and Wells and Squires were committed for trial. The proceedings, partly before Henry Fielding the novelist, were conducted with a laxity that seems now to be almost inconceivable. At the Old Bailey trial there was a remarkable conflict of evidence, but in the end Mrs. Wells was condemned to be burned in the hand, and Mary Squires to be hanged. Sir Christopher Gascoyne then Lord Mayor, was satisfied that there had been a miscarriage of justice and made enquiries, a respite was obtained and finally the law officers of the crown recommended the grant of a free pardon to Squires. The natural sequel was the prosecution of Canning for perjury. Fortune and Judith Natus now swore that they had slept each night in the loft where Canning declared she had been imprisoned, but it was very natural that people should ask why they had not given this important evidence at the previous trial. Mary Squires, alibi was sworn to by thirty-eight witnesses who had seen her in Dorsetshire, and was, to some extent, invalidated by twenty-seven who swore that she was in Middlesex at the time. As she was too remarkable for her ugliness to be easily mistaken, there must have been some very "hard swearing." Canning was convicted of perjury and transported, but the secret of her absence from New Year's Day, 1553, until the 29th of January was never divulged. The case excited great interest, and the controversy divided the whole of the busy, idle "town," into "Canningites" and "Gipsyites."

The Tudor law (22 Henry VIII., c. 10) was repealed as "of excessive severity" in 1783 (23 George III., c. 51). The later legislation provides that persons wandering in the habit and form of Egyptians, and pretending to palmistry and fortune-telling, are to be deemed rogues and vagabonds (17 Geo. II., c. 5., 3 Geo. IV., c. xl.), and is liable to three months' imprisonment (5 Geo. IV., c. lxxxiii.), and encamping on a turnpike road involved a penalty of forty shillings (3 Geo. IV., c. cxxvi., 5 and 6 William IV., c. 50). Some of the older enactments remained on the statute book, though not enforced, until the passing of the statute law Revision Act of 1863, by which many obsolete parliamentary enactments were swept away.

By the famous Poynings Act, English laws were declared applicable to Ireland. The gipsies were never common in the Isle of Saints, but by a special act they were, in 1634, declared to be rogues and vagabonds (10 and 11 Car. I., c. 4).

There are acts of the Scottish Parliament as early as 1449, directed against "sorners, overliers, and masterful beggars with horse, hounds, or other goods," and that this would well describe the earlier gangs of gipsies is undeniable, but whether they were Romanis or Scots is a matter of controversy not easily decided in the absence of more definite evidence. A tradition of the Maclellans of Bombie says that the crest of the family was assumed on the slaying of the chief of a band of saracens or gipsies from Ireland. The conqueror received the barony of Bombie from the king as a reward. Having thus restored the fortunes of the family, the young laird of Bombie took for his crest a moor's head with the motto "Think on." If this legend was evidence, which it is not, there were gipsy marauders in Galloway in the middle of the fifteenth century. But in 1505, we have the entry of a gift by the King of Scotland of seven pounds to the "Egiptianis." In the same year there is a letter already named, in which "Anthonius Gagino," or Gawino, is recommended to the King of Denmark. In 1527, Eken Jacks, master of a band of gipsies, was made answerable for a robbery from a house at Aberdeen. In 1539, a similar charge was brought, but not proved, against certain friends and servants to "Earl George, callet of Egipt." This chieftain was one of the celebrated Faa tribe. In 1540, George and John Faa were ordered by the bailies of Aberdeen to remove their company and goods from the town. This is the first action of a Scottish authority against the gipsies as gipsies. But, by a charter dated four days before the municipal decree, James V. confirms to "our lovit Johnne Faw, lord and erle of Little Egipt," full power to execute justice over his tribe, some of whom had rebelled and forsaken his jurisdiction. In 1541, an act of the Lords of Council and Session decreed the banishment of the gipsies from the realm within thirty days, because of "the gret theftes and scathis" done by them. Some of them passed over the border, but not for long, and in 1553 the Faas again had a charter upholding their rights of lordship against Lalow and other rebels of their company. And in the next year their is a pardon to four Faas for the "slachter of umquhile Ninian Smaill."

The gipsies had the favour of the Roslyn family, and it is said that Sir William Sinclair rescued "ane Egiptian" from the gibbet in the Burgh Muir, "ready to be strangled," and that in gratitude the tribe used to go to Roslyn yearly and act several plays in May and June. In 1573, and again in 1576, the gipsies were ordered to leave the realm, but the decree was never put in force. When Lady Foulis was tried in 1590, one charge was that she had sent a servant to the gipsies for advice as to poison to be administered to "the young laird of Fowles and the young Lady Balnagoune." When James VI. held a High Court of Justicary at Holyrood in 1587, for the reformation of enormities, the offenders to be dealt with included "the wicked and counterfeit thieves and limmers calling themselves Egyptians."

There were several enactments of the Scottish

LAWS RELATING TO THE GIPSIES.   177

Parliament in 1574, 1579, 1592, and 1597. These were all aimed at the nomadic habits of the race, but the settled gipsies were left unmolested. "Strong beggars and their children" were to be employed in common work for their whole life, and it is said that salt masters and coal masters thus made serfs of many. In 1603, there was a special "Act anent the Egiptians," which declared it "lesome" for anyone to put to death any gipsy, man, woman, or child, remaining in the country after a certain date. Moses Faa appealed against it as a loyal subject, and found a security in David, Earl of Crawford. This was in 1609, but in 1611 four of the Faas were tried at Edinburgh under the acts against the gipsies, and were convicted and executed on the same day. Constables and justices of the peace were exhorted to put the law in force. Four gipsies, who could not find securities that they would leave the kingdom, were sentenced to be hanged in 1616, but were reprieved and probably released. In 1624, eight were executed on the Burgh Muir, but the women and children were simply exiled. In 1636, a number were condemned at Haddington, the men to be hanged and *the women to be drowned.* Women who had children were to be scourged and branded in the face. In the latter half of the seventeenth century many were sent to the plantations in Virginia, Barbadoes, and Jamaica.

Generally, however, the stringent laws were not stringently administered, and from fear or influence of some kind the gipsies often escaped.

The British gipsies in our own day find that whilst the law is dealt out to them with perfect impartiality, the social pressure is decidedly against them. At such watering-places as Brighton and Blackpool—to name two extremes —they tell fortunes as though there were no statutes in that case made and provided. But it is not easy for them to keep on the road. The time cannot be far off when they must live with the *gaújos* * as house-dweller or perish from the land.

* *Gaújo* is the name given by the gipsies to all strangers who are not of the Romany race.

Commonwealth Law and Lawyers.

Edward Peacock, f.s.a.

THE great Civil War as it is called, that is the struggle between Charles the First and his parliament, is memorable in many respects. No student of modern history can dispense with some knowledge of it, and the more the better, for it was the result of many things which had happened in the far distant past, and we may safely say that the great French Revolution, which produced some good, and such an incalculable amount of evil would have run a far different course to that which it did, had not the political ideals of the men who took part in that terrible conflict been deeply influenced by what had taken place in England a century and a half before.

As to the civil wars which had occurred in England in previous days, little need be said. They were either dynastic—the struggle of one man or one family against another—or they were religious revolts against the Tudors, by those who vainly endeavoured to re-establish the old order of things in opposition to the will of the reigning monarch and the political servants who supported the throne. The struggle between Charles and the Long Parliament was far different from this. That religion in some degree entered into the conflict which was raging in men's mind long ere the storm burst it would be childish to deny, but it was not so much, except in the case of a very few fanatics, a conflict between different forms of faith as because a great number of the English gentry, and almost the whole of the mercantile class, which had then become a great power, felt that they had the best reasons for believing that it was the deliberate intention of the King and the desperate persons who advised him, to levy taxes without the consent of parliament. This may occasionally have been done in former reigns, but it is the opinion of most of those who have studied the subject in latter days, so far as we can see, without prejudice, that in every case it was illegal. Whether this be so or not, it must be remembered that times were in the days of Charles the First, far different from what his predecessors the Plantagenets and Tudors had known. A

COMMONWEALTH LAW AND LAWYERS. 181

great middle class had arisen partly by the division of property consequent on the dispersion of the monastic lands, and partly also by the break up of the vast feudal estates, some of which had fallen into the hands of the Crown by confiscation, others been sold by their owners to pay for their own personal extravagence.

Though murmurs had existed for many years, it was not until the memorable ship-money tax was proposed that affairs became really grave. Had England been threatened by an invasion such as the Spanish Armada, there can be no doubt that a mere illegality in the mode of levying taxes to meet the emergency would have been regarded as of little account, but in the present case there was no overwhelming need, and it must be borne in mind that to add to the national irritation the two first Stuarts were almost uniformally unsuccessful in their foreign wars. It is to Attorney General Noy that we owe the arbitrary ship-money tax. He was a dull, dry, legal antiquary of considerable ability, whose works, such as his *Treatise concerning Tenures and Estates; The Compleat Lawyer; The Rights of the Crown*, and others of a like character, are yet worth poring over by studious persons. Such a man was well fitted for historical research, no one of his time could have edited and annotated *The Year Books* more efficiently, but he had no conception of the times in which he lived, the narrow legal lore which filled his mind produced sheer muddle-headedness, when called upon to confront an arbitrary king face to face with an indignant people. That there was less to be said against this form of royal taxation than any other that legal ingenuity could light upon must be admitted, but as events shewed the course he advised the king to take, was little short of madness. John Hampden, who represented one of the oldest and most highly respected races of the English gentry—nobles as they would be called in any land but our own—set the example of refusing to pay this unjust levy. The trial lasted upwards of three weeks, and the men accounted most learned in the law were employed in the case. Sir John Bankes, the owner of Corfe Castle, Sir Edward Littleton, and others were for the King. Oliver Saint John and Mr. Holborn were for Hampden. Concerning Holborn little seems to be known, but Saint John made for himself a great name. His speeches are marvellously learned, shewing an amount of reading which is simply wonderful when we call to mind that in those days all our national records were unprinted, and almost all of them without calendar or index of any sort. It must, however, be remembered that in those days lawyers of both branches of the profession were well acquainted not only with the language in which our records were written, but also with the hands employed at various periods, and the elaborate system of contraction used in representing the words.

A full report of this memorable trial is to be found in Rushworth's *Historical Collections*, volume ii. parts 1 and 2. Carlyle in his *Letters and Speeches of Oliver Cromwell*, in the emphatic diction he was accustomed to use says that Saint John was "a dark, tough man of the toughness of leather,"* but he does not dwell on his great learning and general ability, as he ought to have done. That Saint John's heart was in his work for his client we are well assured. That from a legal point of view, Hampden was his only client, we well know, but as a matter of fact, it is no exaggeration to say that he represented the people of England. The decision went in favour

* *Edition* 1857, vol. i., p. 77.

of the crown, which was from the first a foregone
conclusion. It was a legal victory, but like many
lesser victories won before and since success was
the sure road to ruin. The sum contended for
was absurdly small—twenty shillings only—but
on that pound piece hung all our liberties;
whether we were to continue a free people or
whether we were to have our liberties filched
away from us, as had already been the case in
France and Spain. A sullen discontent brooded
over the land, there was no rioting, but in hall
and castle, country parsonage and bar-parlour,
grave men were shaking their heads and asking
what was to come next, all knew that a storm
was brewing, the only question was when and
where it would burst. Events changed rapidly,
and Saint John though he took no very
prominent part in the party struggles ere the
war broke out, was undoubtedly the chief legal
adviser of those who were in opposition to the
faction which desired to make England a despotic
monarchy. Such was the case during the war
which ended in the tragic death of the king, and
the establishment of a Republican form of
government under the name of the Commonwealth. Saint John once again appears in a public

manner which indicates that he was a brave man who had no more fear of the pistol and dagger of the assassin, than he had of the corrupt dealings of those who for a time, to their own imminent peril had misgoverned our country. This time we find him sent by the Commonwealth as ambassador to the seven United Provinces, then as now commonly called Holland, on account of the two provinces of north and south Holland, being by far the most influential states in that republic. The Dutch though republicans themselves, had during the latter part of our Civil War shewn sympathy with the cause of the Royalists. After the execution of the king, this feeling became naturally much intensified. On the other hand our newly established republic was for many reasons both of politics and religion very desirous of being on good terms with a sister commonwealth so very near at hand. To explain matters and perhaps to settle the heads of a definite treaty, the English government sent Isaac Doreslaus, or Doorslaer as their ambassador. He was by birth a Dutchman and a very learned lawyer. He had come to this country before, the war broke out in 1642. He was then made, probably through the influence of his friend Sir Henry Mildmay, "Advocate of the Army."* His great knowledge of Civil Law, which had been much neglected in England in times subsequent to the Reformation, rendered him of great service in his new position of Judge Advocate of the Army. For the same reason he soon afterwards was created one of the judges of the Admiralty Court. He became especially hateful to the Royalists from his having assisted in preparing the charges against Charles the First. In May, 1649, he sailed for Holland as Envoy of the English government to the Hague. He had only spent a short time there, when, while at supper in the Witte Zwaan (White Swan) Inn, some five or six ruffians with their faces hidden by masks, rushed into the room where he, in company with eleven other guests were sitting. Two of these wretches made a murderous attack on a Dutch gentleman of the company, mistaking him for Dorislaus. Finding out their error they set upon the Envoy and slew him with many wounds, crying out as they did so, "Thus dies one of the King's judges." The leader of this execrable gang was Col. Walter

---

* Peacock. *Army Lists of Roundheads and Cavaliers*, 2nd edit., 1874, p. 21.

Whitford, son of Walter Whitford, D.D. The murderer received a pension for this "generous action" * after the Restoration.

The English Parliament gave their faithful servant a magnificent funeral in Westminster Abbey, June 14, 1649, but when Charles the Second ascended the throne, his body was disturbed. His dust rests along with that of Admiral Blake and other patriots in a pit somewhere in Saint Margaret's churchyard.† Dorislaus, though a foreigner, ought to rank among our great English lawyers, for his services were devoted entirely to his adopted country. Whatever our opinions may be as to those differences which were the forerunners of so much bloodshed and crime, we must bear in mind that many of the foremost men on both sides were actuated by the highest principles of honour. The study of Canon Law had been prohibited in the preceding century, and the Civil Law with which it has so intimate a connection, though not made contraband, was so much discouraged that it is no exaggeration to say that the knowledge of it was confined to a very few. Selden, whose

* Wood, *Athenae Oxon*, sub nom.
† John Loden Gollpried's *Kronyck*, vol. iv., p. 454. Van der Aa, *Biographisch Woordenbock*, sub voce.

wide grasp of mind took in almost every branch of learning as it was known in his day, is the only English lawyer we can think of who had mastered these two vast subjects. This is the more remarkable as he was of humble parentage; the son of a wandering minstrel it is said, but from the first his passion for learning overmastered all difficulties. It must, however, be borne in mind that according to the custom of those times when his abilities became known, he met with more than one generous patron.

We must for a moment return to Saint John who was selected in 1652, to represent his country in Holland. There was not, as there is now a trained body of men devoted to the diplomatic service. The reasons why Saint John was chosen for this important office are not clear. He was a great and widely read lawyer, who we apprehend was trusted with this difficult mission, not only because the government were assured of his probity, but because the relations between Holland and this country depended on many subtile antiquarian details which a mere student of the laws as they were then, would have been unable to unravel. The basis of the sea codes by which the various nations of christendom pro-

COMMONWEALTH LAW AND LAWYERS. 189

fessed to be ruled, was the Laws of Oleron (Leges Uliarences). They were promulgated by Richard the First of England, on an island in the Bay of Acquitaine. How far they were ever suited for their purpose may be questioned, but it is certain that as centuries rolled on, they had though often quoted, ceased to have any restraining power, and as a consequence Spain, England, Holland, and other powers were guilty of constant acts of what we should now call piracy. A lasting treaty with Holland, could Saint John achieve it, would have been of immense advantage, but the Dutch were in no mood for an alliance on equal terms. It was a brave thing for Saint John to undertake so arduous a mission, for he not only run the risk of ignominous failure, but also was in no little danger from the savage desperadoes who thought they did the cause of their exiled master service by murdering the agents of the English government. When Saint John arrived at the Hague he was put off by slow and evasive answers, which soon shewed to him not only that his own time was being wasted, but what was to him of far more account, the honour of his country was being played with. He gave a proud, short, emphatic reply to the Dutch sophistries, and at once returned home again, to cause the celebrated Navigation Act to be passed, forbidding any goods to be imported into England, except in English ships, or in the ships of the country where the articles were produced. This was well-nigh ruin to the trade of the Dutch, who were then the great carriers of the world.

In no sketch however brief of the lawyers of this disturbed time, can the name of William Prynne be entirely passed over, and yet it is not as a lawyer that his name has become memorable. Had he been a mere barrister at law he would long since have been forgotten, but he was an enthusiastic puritan of the presbyterian order, and a no less enthusiastic antiquary. He had probably read as many old records as Saint John or Selden, but had by no means their faculty of turning them to good account. He first comes prominently before us as attacking the amusements of the court, especially theatrical entertainments. For this he was proceeded against in the Star Chamber, sentenced to pay five thousand pounds and have his ears cut off; for an attack on episcopacy he was fined another five thousand pounds and sentenced once more to have his ears cut off. He afterwards bore a prominent part in the trial of Archbishop Laud. All along he continued to pour forth a deluge of pamphlets. He attacked Cromwell with such boldness, that the Protector felt called upon to imprison him in Dunster Castle, where however, his confinement was of a most easy character. He is said while there to have amused himself by arranging the Lutterell Charters, for which that noble home is famous. He took the side of Charles the Second at the Restoration, and as a reward was made keeper of the records in the Tower, a post for which he was peculiarly well fitted.

There is probably nothing which distinguishes the periods of the Commonwealth and the Protectorate more markedly from other times of successful insurrection, than the very slight alteration which the new powers introduced into the laws of England. The monarchy, it is true, was swept away, but the judges went on circuit; the courts of Chancery and common-law sat as usual, the Lords of Manors held their courts, and the justices of peace discharged their various functions as if they had been the times of profoundest peace. No confiscations took place, as had been the case in the reign of Henry the Eighth and his successor, except in cases where the owners had been engaged in what the state regarded as rebellion, and even with regard to those who had fought in what is known as the first war, almost everyone was let off by a heavy fine. A list of these sufferers may be seen in *A Catalogue of the lords Knights and Gentlemen that have compounded for their Estates (London Printed for Thomas Dring at the Signe of the George in Fleet Street*, neare Clifford's Inne, 1655.) The book is imperfect and very inaccurate. This is not of much consequence however, as the documents from which it is compiled known as *The Royalist Composition Papers*, are preserved in the record office, and are open to all enquirers. Those who madly engaged in what is known as the second war, had their estates confiscated by three acts of parliament of the years 1651 and 1652. These were reprinted and indexed for the *Index Society* in 1879. These latter had their estates given back to themselves or their heirs on the Restoration. It does not seem that those who were fined, except in a very few cases had any return made to them. There have been few civil wars ancient or modern wherein the unsuccessful have been so tenderly treated. Yet sufferings of the poorer classes among the Royalists must have been very great. Next to the arbitrary conduct of the King and those immediately about his person, was the provocation which the Parliamentarians thought that the established church had given, firstly because many of the bishops and clergy maintained an extreme theory of the Divine Right of Kings, which is said first to have been taught in this country by Archbishop Cranmer. If this opinion were really accepted as more than a mere figure of flattering oratory, it made those who complied with it mere slaves to the sovereign, however tyrannical or wicked he might prove himself. The second ground of resentment was that they thought Archbishop Laud and many of the bishops and clergy, concealed Roman Catholics, "disguised Papists," as the common expression ran. We do not believe this charge with regard to Laud or most of the others so rashly accused. We are *quite sure* it was not so if their writings are to be taken as a test of their feelings. Whatever may have been the truth, there is no doubt that even the more tolerant of what may be called the low-church party feared the worst. As early as 11th February, 1629, Oliver Cromwell, who was then member for Huntingdon, made a speech in which he said, "He had heard by relation from one Dr. Beard . . . that Dr. Alablaster had preached flat Popery at Paul's Cross, and that the Bishop of Winchester (Dr. Neale), had commanded him as his Diocesan, he should preach nothing to the contrary."* So inflamed, however, were men's minds that as soon as the Parliamentary party was strong enough, Laud was indicted for high treason and beheaded.

One of the first works of the Parliament when strong enough, was to abolish the *Book of Common Prayer*, and put a new compilation called the *Directory* in its place. The use of the Prayer Book was forbidden not only in public offices of religion, but in private houses also. For the first offence five pounds was to be levied, for the second ten, and for the third the delinquent was to suffer one year's imprisonment.† Whether this stringent law was

---

* Carlyle, *Letters and Speeches* of Oliver Cromwell, vol. i., p. 50.
† Henry Scobell, *Acts and Ordinances*, 1645, chapter 57.

COMMONWEALTH LAW AND LAWYERS. 195

rigorously inforced we cannot tell. Probably in many cases the local justices would be far more lenient to the clergy who were their neighbours, that would be the legislators at Westminster, whose passions were fanned by listening to the popular preachers. Not content with interfering with the service-book, various acts were passed relating to "Scandalous, Ignorant, and Insufficient ministers." That the commissioners who put these acts in force removed some evil persons we do not doubt, but if John Walker's *attempt towards recovering an account of the number and sufferings of the Clergy of the Church of England, who were sequestered . . . in the Grand Rebellion,* be not very grossly exaggerated, which we see no reason, to believe, many innocent persons must have had very hard treatment.

The marriage laws of England were in a vague and unsatisfactory state from the reign of Edward the Sixth, until the Commonwealth time. An attempt was made in 1653 to alter them. Banns were to be published either at Church or in the nearest market town on three market days, after this the marriage was to take place before a justice of peace. Many entries of marriages of this kind are to be found in our parochial registers. English was made the language of the law in 1650, but Latin was restored to the place of honour it had so long held, when the Restoration took place.

Cock=Fighting in Scotland.

IT is highly probable that the Romans introduced cock-fighting into this country. It is generally believed that the sport was made popular by Themistocles. On one occasion he saw two cocks fighting, and their courage greatly impressed him, and he felt such exhibitions might teach a useful lesson of bravery to those who witnessed them. Periodical contests were exhibited, and were popular amongst the Greeks and Romans and with other nations, and were much appreciated by a large section of the inhabitants of this land. In " Bygone England," by William Andrews, F.R.H.S. (London 1892), will be found a long account of "Fighting-Cocks in Schools." One of the earliest accounts of the pastime in England, says Mr. Andrews, occurs in a "Description of the City of London," by William Fitzstephen, who wrote in the reign of Henry II., and died in the year 1191. He records that it was the annual custom on Shrove Tuesday for the boys to bring their game cocks to the schools, to turn the schoolrooms into cockpits, the masters and pupils spending the morning witnessing the birds fighting.

Old town accounts contain many references to this custom, for example at Congleton, Cheshire, is the following item :—

> "1601. Payd John Wagge for dressynge the schoolhouse at the great [Congleton] cockfyghte." - - £0 0s. 4d.

Hugh Miller, the famous geologist, who was born in the year 1802, in his popular volume "My Schools and Schoolmasters," gives a graphic account of that amusement in the Cromarty grammar school where he received his education. "The school," says Miller, "like almost all other grammar schools of the period in Scotland, had its yearly cock-fight, preceded by two holidays and a half, during which the boys occupied themselves in collecting and bringing up the cocks. And such was the array of fighting birds mustered on the occasion, that the day of the festival from morning till night used to be spent in fighting out the battle. For weeks after it had passed, the school floor continued to retain its deeply stained blotches of blood, and the boys would be full of exciting narratives regarding the

COCK-FIGHTING IN SCOTLAND.

glories of gallant birds who had continued to fight until their eyes had been pecked out ; or who in the moment of victory, had dropped dead in the middle of the cock-pit." Miller at some length denounces the cruel sport.

In England cock-fighting is prohibited by statute 12 and 13 Vict. 3, 92, under which every person who shall in any manner encourage, aid, or assist at the fighting or baiting of any bull, bear, badger, dog, cock, or other animal, shall forfeit and pay a penalty not exceeding £5 for every such offence. In Scotland it was not illegal until quite recently. An act was passed in 1850 known as the "Cruelty to Animals (Scotland) Act," but the wording of the statute was found not to include the game or fighting-cock. The sport became popular and the law could not touch those that took part in the cruel amusement. It was felt to be a national scandal, and to prevent it, a short statute was passed on 30th May, 1895, whereby the definition of the word *animal* in the 11th section was amended by adding at the end thereof the words "or any game or fighting-cock, or other domestic fowl or bird."

Mr. Robert Bird, the genial and gifted author

of "Law Lyrics," a volume which has been warmly welcomed by the public and the press, has made cock-fighting the subject of a clever poem.

COCKIELEERIE-LAW.

By Robert Bird.

In Full Court, Edinburgh, 23rd December, 1892.

Six legal wigs, like well-plumed tappit hens,
Sat brooding o'er a pair of fighting cocks ;
While lesser wigs, begowned, and brief in hand,
Declaimed in flowing periods, of the fray,
Like ancient bards, that wanted but their harps,
Their wallets, ballad verse, and song, to make
The very goose quills, sleeping on the bench,
Awake ! take sides and spill each other's ink.
And as they spake, a legal fog dropt down
Upon the learned six, and each beheld,
In green mirage, born of the cloud of words,
Two cocks, Game cocks, crop-combed, erect, and slim,
With feathers dipped in crimson, gold, and blue,
Frill-necked, with trailing wings and spurs of steel,
That on each other flew and pecked and spurred,
And spurred and pecked again, until the Court
Reeked like a cock-pit, and the crowd of wigs,—
Of boyish idle wigs,—took bonnet shapes
That hooded scowling brows of cursing men,
Who laid their bets on this bird, and on that,
As, with quick panting breath and beaks agape,
They pranced, flew, fought, until the oaken bar
Seemed spattered o'er with feathers and cock blood
At length one cock the other overthrew,

COCK-FIGHTING IN SCOTLAND.

And struck quick spurs into his quivering breast
Until he died; then he, with croaking crow,
Fell, wounded, bleeding, dying by his side
Amid the applauding cheers of thirsty throats,
Soon to be slaked with liquid bets, and so
The battle ended, but the fog remained.

A rustling of silk plumes upon the bench,
Five wigs bent low, and thus great Solon spake—
" 'Twas in Kilbarchan that this fight was fought,
And straight the men who prompted it were ta'en,
And jailed, and tried, and sentenced for the same;
But now they seek release, and this their plea,
That in the gracious Act which says that men
Shall not treat brutes and beasts with cruelty,
The name of "*Cock*" is absent; therefore they
Claim full exemption for their brutish deeds,
And we, vicegerents of our gentle Queen,
With spectacle on nose, must well explore
This vital point in *Cockieleerie-law.*

The illumined page of history reveals
Cock-fighting as an ancient royal sport.
The Early Greeks and Romans in their day
Found pastime sweet in setting cock on cock;
The sage Themistocles took keen delight
In battling fowls; while glorious Cæsar, too,
Loved much to back his bird; and, furthermore,
Marc Antony's gamecocks did always lose
When pitted against Cæsar's fiercer breed.
King Henry VIII., of sainted memory!
At Whitehall had a special cock-pit built,
Wherein his royal birds made lively sport
For gentle dames and all his merry knights.
The most accomplished scholar of his day,

Squire Roger Ascham, tutor to Queen Bess,
Much as he loved his books, loved cocks the more,
And loved them most when victors in the fight.
And last of all, that great and noble Duke,
The conqueror of Blenheim, in game birds
Found something that reminded him of self ;
And thus we see the fighting instinct strong
In cocks, and other nobles of past time.

" Game cocks, we find, from earliest Cockereldom,
Delight in war, as dogs to bark and bite,
And raining blows upon each other's ribs
Do best fulfil their part of nature's plan,
Which built them slim and bade them love the fray ;
And while we hope no preference here to show,—
'Tis open question, whether rearing fowls
To wring their necks, or match them in the pit,
Does more exalt the brute or sink the man.

" But here, the cocks were armed with spurs of steel,
And 'tis a subtle matter, whether they
With iron shod, or spurred with native horn,
Do deal the deadliest blows in angry fray ;
And, while we have our own opinion strong !
'Tis not within our province to pronounce.

" If it be wrong with steel to prick a fowl,
What of the spurs with which hard riders goad
The bleeding sides of horses in the race,
Or in the steeplechase, or country hunt ?
And what of hares in coursing run to death ?
Of quivering foxes torn by yelling hounds ?
Of wheeling pigeons slaughtered for a prize ?
We make no mention of the common use,
Of otter hunting, grouse and pheasant drives.

COCK-FIGHTING IN SCOTLAND.

And of the sport termed *noble*, where the stag
Is forced upon the guns that lay him low.
No doubt, two blacks can never make one white,
Nor multiplying blacks turn black to grey ;
But if to brutalise mankind be thought amiss,
Then there are other ways, than fighting cocks.

"Still that's beside our purpose, which is this—
To scan the statute, microscope in hand,
And note if in its sweep humane, we see
A roosting place for fighting chanticleer.
And there we find, or rather fail to find,
The name of "Cock" among the saving list
Of nineteen beasts protected by the law,
Though thus the list concludes, "*and other kinds
Of animals domestic*," or like words.
Are we to find Game Cocks, domestic fowls?
Are we to hold that birds, are animals?
Our view is quite the contrary, or else
There's not a beast, bird, fish, or insect but
The term "domestic" would to them apply,
And make it penal e'en to slay a louse.

"And while, in other parts of this same Act,
We find "Cock" followed by the general phrase,
"*Or other kind of animal*," we hold
It bears not on the matter now in hand,
But only serves to show that Parliament,
When brooding, clucking, hen-like, o'er this Act,
Had Cocks well in their eye, and plainly did,
Of purpose full, omit them from the list ;
And while bear-fights, bull-fights, dog-fights, and all
Vile sports and brutish cruelty to beasts,
The spirit and the letter of the law
Do quite forbid, *unanimous we hold*

*Cock-fighting is a lawful use of Cocks,
And finding so we liberate these men.*

"It will be said, this Statute has been read
Reversely in our sister England, where
It is the Charter of proud Chanticleer;
But what of that? It alters not our mind!
But only shews, that they, of feebler clay,
Stick not at trifles, so the end be good,
And let the heart o'erbeat the legal mind;
While we, of sterner stuff, fail not to find
Motes in the sunshine of their simple wits,
And gnats to strain out of their cups of wine;
For in the nice accomplishment and use
Of splitting hairs, and weighing feathers small,
Of riddling wisdom from a peck of words,
We are more skilled, more subtle, more profound
Than our legal brethren of the South."

Whereat five horse-hair wigs again bowed down
In low obeisance to the mighty sage,
And straight the Court was cleared of cocks and men.

Fatal Links.

By Ernest H. Rann.

A CONSIDERATION of the detection of crime brings forcibly to the mind the fact that officers of law have frequently to depend for success on the accidental discovery of the most trifling items and incidents. Conversely the criminal section of the community who prey on the weakness or folly of their neighbours have to fear not only a knowledge of their principal movements, but the discovery of the connecting link which shall complete the chain of evidence against them. The deepest laid plot, the most cunning scheme, contains a flaw which may be fatal to their operations, to their liberty, and even their life, a flaw which no amount of previous examination may detect, a weakness which can rarely be adequately guarded against. Justice and the vindication of the law, therefore, depend largely on a proper regard being paid to minor occurrences, which at first sight would seem to have no bearing whatever on the particular case under consideration. The history of crime contains numberless instances where the criminal has been brought to justice through one or other of these causes—the presence of particular hairs or threads on his clothing or on the weapon used, the direction of certain cuts on the body of his victim, the possession of trifling articles. At other times dreams have played no inconsiderable part in the vindication of the law, which has also been aided by supernatural visitants, or by the self-consciousness of the criminal.

It would be impossible in a short article like the present to offer a full list of cases of this description, but a few typical instances may be taken with the object of showing how crimes, long hidden, have been discovered in the most remarkable manner. Probably the best example occurred at Augsburg, in 1821. A woman named Maria Anna Holzmann lived in a house in the town belonging to one Sticht. Her means only permitted her to occupy a few of the rooms, and the remaining parts of the premises were let to lodgers, among whom were George Rauschmaier and Joseph Steiner. On Good Friday, April 20th, Holzmann disappeared.

She had not given notice of her intended departure, and nothing was known of it until some days later when Rauschmaier and Steiner also left the premises, saying that their landlady had previously quitted the house, leaving them in possession of her keys. This information, however, was not given to the police until May 17th. In the meantime Holzmann's relatives had become apprehensive of her safety, and being reluctantly forced to the conclusion that foul play had befallen her, they decided to take an inventory of her property, as it was known that, although in humble circumstances, the woman had managed by care and economy to amass considerable wealth. It was found, however, that the greater part of her money and other valuables were missing.

In spite of active enquiries no further action of importance in the matter was possible until the following January, when Theresa Belter, a washerwoman who also lived in the house, announced that she had found a thigh of a human body hidden in the loft. Further investigations revealed a leg and the other thigh in a heap of rubbish in a corner of the room, and between the chimney and the roof, a trunk without head or limbs was discovered. An old gown and a petticoat, identified as portions of the dress of Holzmann, were also brought to light, while search in Rauschmaier's room disclosed other parts of a woman's body. The head was missing, but when news of the unmistakeable crime was noised abroad, a neighbouring manufacturer stated that during the preceding year he had found a skull, still bearing portions of flesh and hair, in his factory weir, but had not considered the "find" worthy of preservation.

There could be no doubt that Maria Anna Holzmann had been murdered, and the whole machinery of the law was put in motion to bring the criminals to justice. Suspicion fastened itself strongly upon the two men, Rauschmaier and Steiner, but actual evidence against them, or indeed against anyone, was of the scantiest description until the separate pieces of the woman's body were placed together. While the left arm was being examined, a brass ring fell out of the bend of the elbow, whence it had evidently slipped from the finger of the murderer. Whose was the ring? then became the all important question. Rauschmaier was arrested and confessed that he had stolen and pawned several articles of Holzmann's property, but he sternly denied having committed the murder. The property, including a pair of ear-rings, had been recovered from the pawnbroker's, and these, with the brass ring, were laid before the accused. He had not wit enough to discern the trap laid for him, and immediately on seeing the ornaments, he exclaimed "The ear-rings and the gold and brass rings are mine. The brass ring I always wore until within four or five weeks after Easter, since when I have worn gold ones. The brass ring fits the little finger of my left hand; it slips on and off with ease." This foolish statement, and the place of the discovery of the ring, proved conclusively that Rauschmaier was the murderer of the unfortunate Holzmann. Subsequently he made full confession of the crime, stating that the brass ring must have slipped off while he was cutting up the body. He paid the penalty of his sins with death.

The "Greenacre" case, which occurred in 1836, was similar to the foregoing in many of its details. In that year, portions of the mutilated trunk of an old woman named Brown were found in a house in Edgeware Road, wrapped in old rags and sacking. Subsequently the head was discovered in Regent's Canal, and the limbs in a drain in the neighbourhood of Camberwell. Comparison between the various portions left no doubt as to the identity of the deceased, and James Greenacre, whom Brown intended to marry, and to whose house she had gone with all her property, was accused of the murder. A woman named Gale with whom he lived was also charged with complicity in the deed. Once more suspicion, however strong, was insufficient to bring the crime right home to the accused, but the discovery, among Greenacre's property, of some rags corresponding with the pieces covering the mutilated remains, together with a few articles belonging to Brown, turned suspicion into actual proof. Greenacre was condemned to death, and his companion sentenced to transportation for life.

The murder of William Begbie, at Edinburgh, is a remarkable case of the manner in which the author of a crime may remain long hidden, and only then be discovered by accident. Begbie was a bank porter, and on November 30th, 1806, he was employed to carry a parcel of notes, worth about £4,000, to one of the bank's customers. On his way he had to pass through a narrow, dark, and tortuous entry, and there he was brutally murdered and the notes were stolen.

Although a knife, of a particular pattern, was left in the body, the murderer remained at large, and no clue to the terrible crime could be unearthed. Nine months later the bundle of notes, untouched, was found hidden in a wall, but long years passed before the mystery was completely solved. In 1822 a Bow Street runner named Denovan, while visiting Leith, chanced to fall into conversation with a sailor lately returned from captivity among the French. Speaking of old times the mariner accidentally mentioned that coming ashore one morning he had noticed a man like William Begbie, followed by a person dressed in black and of respectable demeanour. He lost sight of them for a few moments, but later on he was surprised to see the man in black rush out of the narrow entry with a bundle under his arm. On the next day he heard of the murder, and feeling confidant that he could throw light on the crime, he informed the mate of his vessel of what he had seen. Permission to go ashore was, however, refused. The vessel sailed, was captured by the French, and the sailor witness did not recover his liberty for fifteen years. Denovan set to work with this important clue, and enquiries proved that the man in black was no other than a notorious criminal named Mackoul, who had lived in Edinburgh in 1806. The law had claimed its own, however, previous to the sailor's disclosures. In 1820 Mackoul had suffered death for robbery; still, though he was beyond punishment for his old crime in Edinburgh, it was satisfactory to know that the mystery of the bank porter's death had at last been solved.

Probably the most notorious case in English annals of murder discovered by extraordinary means is that of the killing of Daniel Clarke by Eugene Aram. The main facts of the case are so well known that it is scarcely necessary to enter into them here. Aram, assisted by a man named Houseman, it may be remembered, murdered Clarke for the sake of his wealth, and hid the body in St Robert's cave, near Knaresborough. There it remained from 1745 till 1759, when it was accidentally discovered by a labourer. Close examination led to the conclusion that the body, or rather the skeleton, was that of a murdered man, and when the mysterious and almost forgotten disappearance of Clarke was remembered, steps were taken to arrest his quondam companions Aram and Houseman. The latter turned king's evidence, and on his testimony Aram was executed, leaving a shady memory to be invested with undeserved romance by a poet and a novelist of the following century.

Researches into modern criminal records also reveal a number of interesting cases similar to those cited above. A few years ago a Pole named Lipski was convicted in London of the murder of a woman. Strenuous efforts were made to obtain a pardon, on the ground that he had been wrongly convicted, but the solitary fact on which the Home Secretary decided to allow the law to take its course was that the door of the room had been locked in which the woman was found murdered, with Lipski himself hiding under the bed. And in tracing the Muswell Hill murder to its authors, the police were aided in their endeavours by the discovery of a common lantern which had been left on the scene of the crime. It was supposed to belong to a relative of one of the suspected men, and in order to verify this important link in the chain of evidence, a youthful agent of the detective force was employed to spin his top in front of the supposed owner's house, engage him in conversation if possible, and obtain evidence of the ownership of the lantern. The result was completely satisfactory; the suspicions of the police were confirmed, and the murderers brought to justice, mainly, it may be said, through the lantern's silent testimony.

Another case of murder, which occurred in 1806, was brought home in a singular and complete manner. A Deptford gentleman, named Blight, was killed by a pistol-shot, and Sir Astley Cooper, from an examination of the victim's wounds and of the place of his murder, arrived at the opinion that none other than a left-handed man could have committed the crime. Acting on this conclusion the police arrested one Patch, who had been seen in the locality. When Patch was asked to hold up his hand to plead the indictment, he put up his left hand. The jury brought in a verdict of guilty, and before execution the criminal made full confession of his terrible deed.

Dreams also have played no inconsiderable part in the discovery of crime. We have not space in the present article to notice all trials where dream-evidence has been offered to the court; a brief notice of those cases in which it has had an important bearing must suffice. The most notorious instance, of course, is that of Maria Martin, the victim of the Red Barn tragedy. After her departure from home, in order, as was supposed, to marry William Corder, nothing, either by way of letters, or otherwise, was heard of her, except brief mention in Corder's communications. Nearly twelve months passed, when Mrs. Martin was startled and horrified by dreaming, on three successive nights, that Maria had been murdered and buried in the Red Barn. After much persuasion her husband and son consented to search the place, and there, in the exact spot indicated by Mrs. Martin as having been pointed out in her dreams, was found the body of her missing daughter, buried under the flooring in a sack.

Mention may also be made of the case of Ulick Maguire, an Irish farmer, whose wife dreamed that her husband had been murdered by a disappointed lover of hers, named O'Flanagan. A few days later an idiot boy, who lived in the house, was heard shrieking in terror: "Shanus dhu more O'Flanagan (big black James) has kilt Ulick, and buried him under the new ditch at the back of the garden. I dhramed it last night, evry wurrd av it." The singular coincidence of the lad's dream with her own excited Mrs. Maguire's suspicions to the utmost, especially as her husband was away from home at the time. She ordered a search at the particular spot mentioned by the idiot boy, and there, to her horror, was found the body of Ulick, with the skull cleft in twain. Immediate request was made for "big black James." He had absconded and enlisted in the army, but on being charged with the crime he admitted his guilt, and suffered the penalty of death.

In one instance, by far the most wonderful of its kind, the victim of a murder has appeared in successive dreams, and played the part of detective with admirable skill and effectiveness. A Grub Street victualler, named Stockton, was murdered towards the close of the seventeenth century. Three men were suspected of the crime, but neither of them could be discovered, and the affair seemed likely to become one of the mysteries of crime, when a Mrs. Greenwood dreamed that Stockton, who had been a neighbour during life, had taken her to a house in Thomas Street, telling her that his murderer was inside. On going to the house in person Mrs. Greenwood was told that Maynard, one of the suspected men, had gone abroad. The following night Stockton appeared and showed her the features of Maynard, and gave her such particulars of the

FATAL LINKS. 217

man's habits and resorts that he was captured within a few hours. From Maynard the names of his partners in guilt, Bevel and Marsh, were obtained, but again the authorities were at fault, until Stockton indicated the house where Marsh visited, and the yard (afterwards discovered to be the yard of Marshalsea Prison) in which Bevel would be found. From a crowd of other prisoners Mrs. Greenwood identified Bevel, and shortly afterwards, through her strange testimony, Marsh also was arrested. Then, as an old chronicle of the case affirms, Stockton appeared for the last time, and thanked her for her good offices. We have given the story as it has come down through two centuries; a whole body of clergymen attested its accuracy at the time, and present-day enquirers would have great difficulty, we imagine, in conclusively proving that the murder of Stockton was traced by other and less extraordinary means.

Closely allied to the evidence furnished by dreams, and indeed, as in the foregoing case of Stockton, sometimes barely distinguishable from it, is that offered by ghosts, actually seen by witnesses in a waking, but hallucinatory, state. Such evidence would scarcely be admissable in modern courts of law, but in past ages it was freely employed, and has served to bring criminals to the gallows. It must be admitted that the other testimony against the accused was strong, but in numerous instances ghosts have been instrumental in putting the officials on to a clue or track which they would most likely never have discovered by their own unaided efforts. In his "History of Durham," Surtees mentions the case of Anne Walker, who lived in 1630, and had become engaged in an intrigue with a relative of the same name. The girl was placed for a time under the care of a friend in a neighbouring village, but one night she was removed from there by Walker and a man named Sharp. From that date no one saw her alive. A fortnight afterwards, Graime, a fuller, was terrified by the appearance in his mill of Anne Walker's ghost, "dishevelled, blood-stained, and with five wounds in her head." She told him the whole story of her murder; how Sharp had killed her with a collier's pick, and then thrown her body down a shaft. Graime hesitated to use this strangely acquired information. Apparently incensed at his delay, Anne Walker repeatedly appeared, and in order to rid himself of these visitations, the frightened fuller at length acquainted the authorities with his story. Immediate enquiry confirmed his statements in every particular. Walker and Sharp were arrested, charged with the murder of the girl, found guilty, and executed, though to the last they maintained their innocence of the crime.

A case, somewhat similar, has occurred even in the present century, and in matter-of-fact, new world Australia, where visions might be expected to be few and far between. The friends of a well-to-do settler near Sydney were surprised to hear from his steward that he had been suddenly called to England on important legal business. Remembering the vast wealth of the man, and the necessity for precautions in regard to it, they accepted the statement, and also recognised the steward's control of the estate during his master's absence. What was the astonishment, however, of one of these friends, when on riding over the estate he saw the owner, whom he thought to be in England, sitting on a neighbouring stile? The figure looked at him silently and sorrowfully, then walked towards a pond and disappeared. Drags were procured and the water searched, when the body of the absent owner was brought to the surface. Confronted with the corpse the steward confessed that he had murdered his master at the identical stile on which the ghost had sat.

Pierre le Loyer, a French writer on law and the supernatural, mentions in his "Discours des Spectres," the case of a man who mysteriously vanished, having, as was supposed, been murdered. A few weeks later the ghost of the absentee appeared to his brother, took him to a lonely spot, and there pointed out where he had been murdered and buried by his own wife and her lover. Enraged at this domestic perfidy and wickedness the brother denounced his sister-in-law, and on his testimony she was condemned to be strangled and her body afterwards burned.

About half a century ago a peculiar case of fraud was disclosed by remarkable means during the hearing of a law-suit in Tuscany. The decision of the court turned on the point whether a certain word had been erased from a particular document of importance. Chemical processes were alleged to have been employed, and acting on scientific knowledge one of the lawyers proposed that the document should be heated, as thereby a slight difference of shade or colouring between the paper and the letters supposed to have been removed might become visible. Permission was given to try the experiment, and on the application of heat the important word in question immediately appeared, and the court gave a verdict in accordance with this ingeniously devised testimony.

Since that time the progress and development of science have enabled criminal investigation to be conducted by methods which would otherwise be impossible, and with almost unerring certainty and decision. The microscope and the spectroscope have been employed in numerous cases of murder and forgery where less subtle means of discovery would have proved useless; chemical analysis has become an important agent of detection, while photography has also rendered signal service in the cause of justice. We may not have concerned ourselves with the numerous methods by which bank-note forgeries are detected; hitherto our references have been mainly to the more serious crime of murder, and with a few instances of this character brought to light through modern science our list must close.

Although, generally speaking, the microscope cannot discern any difference between the blood of man and that of other mammalia, yet the merest examination suffices to show the difference between mammalian blood and that of birds, reptiles, or fishes. In the one case the red blood corpuscles are round, and without a nucleus; in the other they are oval and nucleated. On this fact the evidence for a prisoner at Chelmsford charged with murder was completely rebutted. Blood stains had been found on his clothes, which, according to his counsel, had been caused by chicken's blood. But the prosecution brought forward a microscopist, who stated that the blood stains were mammalian, and on this testimony the plea of the prisoner was rejected. In the following year, and at the same assizes, the testimony against a man charged with murder was strengthened by the microscopical discovery of cotton fibres on a certain weapon, which he was said to have used, while the murderers of a man who had been kicked to death were convicted on the evidence of two doctors, who found on the boots of the accused a number of hairs corresponding with the hair on the head of the victim. Evidence of this kind is becoming of extreme importance. Hardly a serious crime is investigated without the application of one or other of these scientific methods of detection, and with each success the career of the criminal becomes increasingly difficult and arduous, and his chances of success more remote. Of remarkable discoveries of crime the microscope, the camera, and the spectroscope furnish the most subtle instances, and it is quite possible that before long other methods of investigation, founded on the most recent scientific achievements, will also be brought into operation. The phonograph and the Röntgen rays are only waiting their turn to serve in the cause of justice.

Post-Mortem Trials.

By George Neilson.

IT might be thought that a man's death made an end of him, and that his mere body had no rights or duties except that of getting decently buried. The middle age had other ideas. The dead still had status and duties. Continental laws recognised acts of renunciation in which a widow laid the keys on her husband's corpse, or tapped his grave with the point of a halberd. The body of a murdered person, or, it might be his hand merely, might be carried before the judge to demand vengeance. * By English thirteenth century law † legal possession of real estate was thought to remain in a man, not until he died, but until his body was borne forth to burial. The dead might be a very potent witness, as shewn by the ordeal of bier-right, ‡ a practice founded on the belief that the murderer's touch

---

* " Michelet's History of France," viii., ch. 1. " Cheruel's Dictionnaire des Institutions," art. " Cadavre."

† " Pollock and Maitland's History of English Law," ii., 60. Bracton 51b, 262.

‡ " Lea's Superstition and Force " (ed. 1892), 359-70.

would cause the victim's wounds to bleed afresh. Thus variously qualified to act as witness or prosecutor as occasion required, it is not surprising to find the dead as defendant also. English history* remembers the strange scene enacted in the monastery of Caen in 1087, when William the Conqueror lay dead there, and the ceremonials of his interment were interrupted by a weird appeal. Ascelin, the son of Arthur, loudly claimed as his, neither sold nor given, the land on which the church stood, and, forbidding the burial, he appealed to the dead to do him justice. More than one† old English poem turned its plot round the ancient canon law, by which a burial might be delayed for debt. The dead was arrestable : a law afterwards set aside, "for death dissolved all things." But in more codes than one death did not dissolve liability for the consequences of high treason.

In Scotland,‡ in the year 1320, at the "black parliament" of Scone, several Scotsmen were convicted of conspiracy against King Robert the

---

* "Roman de Rou," ii., 9320-40.
† "Three Metrical Romances" (Camden Socy.), xxvi., 33. See "Decretals of Gregory," lib. ii., tit. 28, cap. 25, *qua fronte;* also "Lyndwood's Provinciale," p. 278.
‡ "Bower's Scotichronicon," ii., 275. "Extracta e Cronicis," 150. "Scalacronica," 144.

Bruce. Most of them were drawn, hanged, and beheaded. But a Scottish historian of the time tells us that Roger of Mowbray, one of the accused, having died before his trial, "his body was carried to the place, convicted of conspiracy, and condemned to be drawn by horses, hung on the gallows, and beheaded." It is to the credit of Bruce that he did not allow the corporal part of the sentence to be carried out, although many entries in the charter rolls* shew that the consequent escheats of the traitor's lands served to reward the loyalty of others. His body convicted of conspiracy! How came this singular procedure into Scottish practice?

In England, towards the close of the fourteenth century, although escheats were not less keenly looked after than in Scotland—and that sometimes in cases† where men had died unconvicted,—the purpose of attainder appears to have been effected without the expedient of calling the dead to the bar. The dead, however, was convicted. In the case of Robert Plesyngton, ‡ for instance, in 1397, the judgment of Parliament bore an express conviction of treason, "*noun-obstant la mort de dit*

---

* "Robertson's Index," 5, 10, 12, 19, 20, 21.
† "Rolls of Parliament," ii., 335.
‡ "Rolls of Parliament," iii., 384.

POST-MORTEM TRIALS. 227

Roberd." In 1400, John, Earl of Salisbury, challenged for treason by Lord Morley, was killed before the day appointed for the duel. The court not only adjudged him a traitor,[*] but on grounds eked out by Roman law subjected his sureties in costs to his accuser—said costs including the handsome fee of 100s. and twelve yards of scarlet cloth to the lawyer Adam of Usk. [†]

In all features save perhaps that of the actual presence of the body in the trial, warrant can be found for the Scottish practice in Roman law. The offence of "majesty," or high treason, formed an exception to the great humane general rule that responsibility for crime ended with the criminal's breath. Under the Lex Julia [‡] death was no defence to a charge of "majesty;" proceedings could be raised to stamp the dead man's name with the brand of treason; his kinsmen might if they chose deny and defend; but if they failed to clear him his goods were confiscated and his memory damned. There is in the annals of Rome at least one instance § of a death-

[*] "Rolls of Parliament," iii., 459.
[†] "Chronicle of Adam of Usk," pp. 44, 45.
[‡] "Justinian's Institutes," iv., 18. "Digest," xlviii., 4, 11. "Code," ix., 8.
§ "Tacitus," xvi., 11.

sentence of this sort pronounced after the accused was in his grave. Nor was its scope confined absolutely to high treason. The Church had a quiet way of appropriating tit-bits of barbaric policy for pious uses. The Emperor Theodosius * said that the inquisition for heresy ought to extend to death itself; and as in the crime of majesty, so in cases of heresy, it should be lawful to accuse the memory of the dead. The Popes endorsed the analogy, † for heretics had goods, which sometimes were worth forfeiting. The spiritual authority however was of more moment. The Church claimed the power to bind and loose even after death, ‡ and a Welsh twelfth century bishop did not stand alone when he carried it so far as to scourge the body of a king who had died excommunicate. § On the same principle dead heretics—dead before sentence of heresy— were burnt. ‖

It was by a close following up of Roman jurisprudence, with, peradventure, some added light from the law and practice of the Church, that

---

* "Code," i., 5, 4.   † "Decretals of Gregory," v., 7, 10.
‡ "Decretals of Gregory," v., 39, 28.   "Lea's Studies in Church History," 264-66.
§ "Haddan and Stubbs's Councils," i., 393.   "Lea's Studies," 384, 425.
‖ "Lea's Chapters from the Religious History of Spain," 372, 492.

the French devised their *procés au cadavre*,* by which the memory of a dead traitor was attacked. Its special application was to lesemajesty described as divine and human, the former an elastic term covering offences against God and religion. Allied to this latter category, though not exactly of it, was the mortal sin of suicide. Self-slaughter was so deeply abhorrent to mediæval thought as not only to be reckoned more culpable, but to call for more shameful punishment, than almost any other crime. So coupling the traitor and the self-slayer in the same detestation, the law assailed both by the same strange post-mortem process, and (by methods of reasoning which Voltaire was one of the first to ridicule) consigned their souls to perdition, their memories to infamy, and their bodies to the gibbet.† The treatment of the suicide was peculiar in its refinements of symbolic shame. The body was, by the customary law (for example, of Beaumont‡), to be drawn to the gibbet as cruelly as possible, *pour monstrer*

---

* "Cheruel's Dictionnaire," and "Denisart's Collection de Decisions, art. " Lesemajeste, memoire, suicide."

† For a curious English case of gibbetting a suicide in 1234, see "Maitland's Bracton's Note Book," 1114: compare " Bracton," fo. 150.

‡ " La Loy de Beaumont" (Reims 1864), p. 241.

l'experience aux aultres. The very door-step of the house in which he lay was to be torn up, for the dead man was not worthy to pass over it. Impalement, transfixture by a stake, though well enough known on the continent as a punishment of the living, became there and in England alike, the special doom of the suicide. Yet the *procés au cadavre* had no footing in English law, and although it was already in 1320 received in Scotland, we shall find reason for thinking it not wholly welcome.

After the trial in 1320 before alluded to, the records in Scotland are silent for over two centuries, and it is not until 1540 that the process is heard of again. In that year * the heirs of one Robert Leslie were summoned to the court of parliament to hear his name and memory "delete and extinct," for certain points and crimes of lesemajesty, and his lands and goods forfeited to the king. Legal authorities, † obviously forgetful of the fourteenth century instance, follow one another in the mistake of regarding Leslie's as the first of its kind. The legality of the

---

* "Acts of Parliament, Scotland," ii., 356.
† "Mackenzie's Criminal Law," i., 6, 21-2. "Hume's Law of Crimes i., 539. "Pitcairn's Criminal Trials," ii., 278. "Riddell's Scottish Peerages," ii., 757-58.

procedure was called in question at the time. Indeed, so loud was the murmur that it can still be heard in the act passed to put it to silence. "It is murmurit," says the enactment, "that it is ane noveltie to rais summondis and move sic ane actioun aganis ane persoun that is deide, howbeit the commoun law directly providis the samin."* The three estates of parliament therefore on the motion of the lord advocate, declared unanimously "all in ane voce, but † variance or discrepance," that the cause was just and conform to common law. In another case of the following year ‡ the charge and judgment were enrolled in the Acts of Parliament. The widow and the heir of the late James Colville were summoned "to see and hear that the said deceased James, whilst he lived had committed the crime of lesemajesty." The deliverance of parliament as tribunal was by its terms an actual sentence upon the dead—"that the deceased James "hes incurrit the panis of crime of lesemajeste" for which causes the court decerned "the memoure of the said umquhile James to be deleit," and his possessions confiscated to the crown.

* "Acts Parl. Scot.," ii., 356. † *But* = without.
‡ "Acts Parl. Scot.," ii., 369.

Parliament which had unanimously voted the procedure well based in law, found that it was dangerous. It was necessary to restrict its scope. In 1542, it is on parliamentary record* that "the lordis thinkis the said act [*i.e.*, of 1540], ower generale and prejudiciale to all the barions of this realme." This would never do :—an act prejudicial to the barons! So it became statute law in 1542, that it should apply only to cases of grave treason, public and notorious during the offender's life, and that prosecution for the future must be raised within five years after the traitor's death. It was a reasonable restraint, not always observed.

During the reigns of Mary and James VI. a number of trials occurred in which this singular process was resorted to, and in some, if not all, of which the body of the dead appeared at the bar. Occasionally it was embalmed for the purpose. † It had been a part of the border code, prevalent on the marches of England and Scotland, that an accused should, although dead, be brought to the place of judgment in person. In 1249, the marchmen of both realms had declared the law in

* "Acts Parl. Scot.," ii., 415.
† Case of Earl of Huntly in 1562. Tytler's "Hist. of Scotland," iii., 167.

that sense. They said that, in any plea touching life and limb, if the defendant died the body of him should be carried to the march on the day and to the place fixed between the parties, because—concludes this remarkable provision*— "no man can excuse himself by death.." And in the end of the sixteenth century the borderers had not forgotten the tradition their forefathers had inherited in the thirteenth, for in 1597, when Scotsmen and Englishmen were in fulfilment of their treaty obligations presenting their promised pledges, the custom was scrupulously observed on the English side. All were there,—all, though all included one that was no more.† "Thoughe one of the nomber were dead, yet was he brought and presented at this place." They evidently believed on the borders, which Sir Robert Cary with some reason called ‡ an "uncristned cuntry," that a man could best prove that he was dead by attendance in person.

In trials for treason this principle was pushed in some instances to strange extremes. Probably one underlying reason of this, at a date so late, was to make sure that no formality should be

* "Acts Parl. Scot.," i., 415.
† "Bain's Calendar of Border Papers," ii., 417.
‡ "Border Papers," ii., 711.

lacking to make the forfeiture effective. But the main reason one must believe lay in its being a traditional observance. In the trial in 1600, of the Earl of Gowrie and his brother for an alleged attempt on the king's life, the privy council on the preamble * that it was necessary to have their corpses kept and preserved unburied, issued an act to that effect, and the treasurer's accounts contain an entry "for transporting of the corpis of Gowrie and his brother." Their bodies were accordingly produced at the trial, and the sentence which pronounced them guilty of treason and lesemajesty during their lifetime, declared † their name, memory, and dignity extinguished, and ordained that "the dead bodeis of the saidis Treatouris," should be hanged, quartered, and gibbetted. Their "twa hedis," a grim diarist ‡ tells, were set upon the tolbooth, "thair to stand quhill § the wind blaw thame away."

The last case ‖ in the annals, in which this revolting Scottish "practick" was put into effect, occurred in 1609. Robert Logan, of Restalrig,

---

* Pitcairn's Crim. Trials," ii., 233, 241.

† Pitcairn, ii., 167-8. "Acts Parl. Scot.," iv., 199.

‡ "Birrel," quoted in "Pitcairn," ii., 247. § *Quhill*, until.

‖ For an example in 1603, that of Francis Mowbray, see "Pitcairn," ii., 406-9.

had been nearly three years in his grave when it was given out that he had been a party to the alleged Gowrie conspiracy against King James. A process * was at once taken in hand to proscribe his memory and escheat his property. As death was no excuse, neither was burial; and the ghastly form was gone through of exhuming the bones for presentation at the trial. It was a case plainly within the exception provided for in the act of 1542, for the man was not "notourly" a traitor, he had died in repute of loyalty : but the Crown was eager for a conviction. Much incredulity had been rife with regard to the Gowrie conspiracy. The evidences now adduced were—on the surface at any rate, although, perhaps, as many critics still think, on the surface only,—circumstantial and strong. The prosecution was therefore keenly pressed, and the reluctance of some of the judges overcome. A jocular jurist-commentator on these post-mortem trials, has remarked † that the bones of a traitor could neither plead defences, nor cross-question witnesses. But in the dawn of the seventeenth century they could turn the sympathy

---

* A full account of the trial is given in "Pitcairn," ii., 276-92.
† Lord Hailes quoted in "Pitcairn," ii., 277.

of the court against the charge, as it appears they did in Logan's case. The proofs, however, looked overwhelming, and the forfeiture was carried without a dissenting voice from the bench—from the bench, because it was, as all Scots treason-trials then were, a trial by judges only, not by judge and jury. Logan's memory was declared extinct and abolished, and his possessions forfeited. The judgment, however, wreaked no vengeance on the exhumed remains. Humanity was asserting itself even in the trial of the dead, and that institution itself was doomed. Although in disuse ever after, it did not disappear from the theory of law until 1708, when the act 7 Anne, chapter 21, prescribing jury-trial for treason, assimilated the Scots law on the subject to that of England, and thus brought to an unregretted end one of the most gruesome of legal traditions.

Island Laws.

By Cuming Walters.

A VERY curious and interesting phase of self-government is that which is supplied by the independent legal system established in various small islands in the United Kingdom. It is amusing to notice these little communities on rocky islets tenaciously preserving their ancient privileges, and revelling in the knowledge that they have a code of their own by no means in harmony with the statute law of the country of which they are an insignificant part. The tribunals and the legal processes in the Channel Islands, in the Scilly Islands, in the Isle of Man, and even in some of the smaller islands round the English coast, differ entirely from those established in the motherland; and any suggestion of change is warmly resented. In many cases it has not, of course, been worth while to insist on reform, inasmuch as the islands are inhabited only by a few families, who may be left in peace to settle their own differences if any occur.

There are a great many scattered islets about the sinuous line of Irish coast, very few of which are ever visited by strangers. The conditions of life in these isolated places are seldom investigated, and yet we find there are some remarkable survivals of old customs and relics of ancient laws. The people are independent, because they feel they are totally separated from the mainland, and possess neither the means nor the desire to cross over to it. They are in many respects a race by themselves, and their attachment to their little homes of rock is such that one of their severest punishments for offenders is to transport them to Ireland. Such an island is Raghlin, or Rathlin, six miles distant from the north-west of Antrim, but might be six hundred miles, judging by the slight intercourse the handful of inhabitants has with the larger world. Another such island is Tory, ten miles from the Donegal coast, where up to a few years ago the dwellers were unacquainted with any other law than that of the Brehon code. A visitor in 1834 found them choosing their own judge, and yielding ready obedience to mandates "issued from a throne of turf." In this case, and in the case of the Cape Clear islanders, it was found that the threat of banishment to the mainland was severe enough to prevent serious crime. These feelings probably have been modified in more recent times, yet the intensity of the attachment of islanders to their native rock is one of the ineradicable characteristics which account for the sturdy independence manifested in their laws and customs. Their little homes are miniature worlds which they prefer to govern themselves in their own way. We may take the Scillies as a favourable example, where the natives cling to the system of civil government by twelve principal inhabitants forming a Court presided over by a military officer. The Court is held every month, and it has jurisdiction in civil suits and minor causes. The Sheriff for Cornwall has, or, at all events, had, no jurisdiction in the islands, though persons prosecuted for felonies (which are extremely rare) have to be relegated to the Assizes at Launceston.

The patriarchal system has always been much in evidence in the small Scotch islands, which, for the most part, are the possessions of the descendants of feudal chieftains. Dr. Johnson adverted to this fact on the occasion of his famous journey in the North:—"Many of the smaller islands have no legal officers within them.

I once asked, if a crime should be committed, by what authority the offender could be seized, and was told that the laird would exert his right; a right which he must now usurp, but which merely necessity must vindicate, and which is therefore yet exercised in lower degrees by some of the proprietors when legal process cannot be obtained." But after observing how the system operated, Dr. Johnson freely admitted that when the lairds were men of knowledge and virtue, the convenience of a domestic judicature was great. Owing to the remoteness of some of the islands and the difficulty of gaining access to others, it was scarcely possible to bring them under the common law, and we find that in some instances the proprietors were allowed to act as magistrates by the Lord-Lieutenant's commission. Some of the old lairds had a very effective but unjudicial method of enforcing their laws. Lord Seaforth, High Chief of Kintail, was anxious to abolish a very odious custom of woman-servitude which prevailed in the island of Lewis. The men were wont to use the women as cattle, compelling them to draw boats like horses, and, among other things, to carry men across the deep and dangerous fords on their backs. This practice greatly disgusted

Lord Seaforth, who found, however, that it was one particularly hard to check. He arrived one day on horseback at a stream which a peasant was contentedly crossing, mounted on a woman's shoulders. When the middle of the stream was reached, the laird urged his horse forward, and came up with the couple, when by vigorously laying his whip about the back of the man, he compelled him to dismount, and wade as best he could to the opposite bank. This practical indication of the laird's wishes aided considerably in producing a change.

The Scotch islanders are a law-abiding people, and patriarchal government sufficed. It was recorded of the inhabitants of Skye that, during a period of unusual distress and semi-starvation, not a single sheep was stolen. So keen is the sense of propriety in that island that a whole family has been known to slink away, unable to bear the disgrace brought upon them by an individual delinquent. Orkney and Shetland once possessed all the characteristics of a separate kingdom, the laws of no other countries being imposed upon them. There was none to dispute the laird's right, and legal administration was entirely in his hands, except for the period that the islands were placed under episcopal rule. It is worth noting that the most famous of the governing bishops, Robert Reid (*tempus* 1540), also filled the high office of President of the Court of Session at Edinburgh, and he and his successors are said to have ruled with conspicuous mildness and equity.

We may now turn to one or two English islands before devoting attention to the most important examples of all—those supplied by the Isle of Man and the Channel Islands. The Isle of Wight is only regarded as "separate" from Hampshire for one legal purpose, so far as I have been able to ascertain. It is part of the "county of Southampton" for all purposes except the land-tax payment: for this it has a separate liability. But the land-tax divisions are the most irregular, and the least uniform of any legal divisions in the country, and it is therefore not surprising that the Isle of Wight should in this respect be subject to peculiar usage. Purbeck is one of those "isles" in England which now depend more upon tradition for their designation, than natural accordance with the geographical definition. What is remarkable is that these "isles"—such as the Isle of Purbeck, the Isle of

Ely, the Isle of Glastonbury, and the Isle of Meare—nearly all have certain well-established and recognised laws of their own for the little communities which dwell within their borders. The quarrymen of Purbeck consider themselves a race apart, and their guild is one of the closest and strictest character. Their homage is paid exclusively to the lord of the manor, and the "Marblers" claim to have received a special charter from King Edward. On Shrove Tuesday they elect their officers, and celebrate the occasion by kicking a football round the boundaries. One ancient custom observed on these occasions is to carry a pound of pepper to the lord of the manor, as an acknowledgement to him in respect to a "right of way." Until comparatively recent times the government of the island was patriarchal in character. The Isle of Glastonbury had its "House of Twelve Hides" for the trial of petty cases in the locality, and tradition reports that unusually large dungeons were prepared for the immuring of those who offended in the renowned Avalonian isle.

The Isle of Man, when subject to the Kings of Norway, was a subordinate feudatory kingdom. It afterwards came under the dominion of the

English Kings, John and Henry III., but passed afterwards to the Scotch. Henry IV. eventually claimed the little isle, and disposed of it to the Earl of Northumberland, but upon this famous nobleman's attainder it went to Sir John de Stanley. Its government seemed destined to be unsettled, however, and though the title of king was renounced by the possessors of the land, they maintained supreme and sovereign authority as to legal process. In the Isle of Man no English writ could be served, and as a result it became infested with smugglers and outlaws. This was unsatisfactory, and, in 1765, the interest of the proprietor was purchased, in order that the island should be subject to the regulations of the British excise and customs.

According to Blackstone, than whom there could be no greater authority, the Isle of Man is "a distinct territory from England, and is not governed by our laws; neither doth an Act of Parliament extend to it unless it be particularly named therein." It is consequently a convenient refuge for debtors and outlaws, while its own roundabout and antiquated methods of procedure have been found to favour the criminal rather than to aid prosecutors and complainants." Perhaps this was never more vividly illustrated than in the recent case of the murderer Cooper, who profited by the cumbrous and lenient processes of Manx law to the extent of getting an atrocious crime reduced to manslaughter. The laws have often been amended. Prior to 1417 they were "locked up in the breasts of the Deemsters," but Sir John Stanley found that so much injustice was being done under the pretence of law, that he ordered a promulgation to be made. But "breast laws" continued to be administered for another two centuries, until Lord Strange, in 1636, commanded that the Deemsters should "set down in writing, and certify what these breast laws are." In 1777, and also in 1813, the laws of the island were again amended, and every criminal was allowed three separate and distinct trials before different bodies. First the High Bailiff hears his case, then the Deemster and six jurymen, and, thirdly, if he has been committed for trial, he is brought before the Governor and the Deemsters. By the time the case gets to the final court it has usually been "whittled down" to the smallest possible proportions, and doubts have often been raised whether justice is not marred by misplaced and unwarranted lenity. Another strange practice is that the Manx advocates combine the parts of barrister and attorney. The law is hard upon debtors, who can be lodged as prisoners in Castle Rushen, if it is suspected that they are about to leave the island; but there are no County Courts. On the other hand, there are Courts of Law of almost bewildering variety—the Chancery Court, the Admiralty, the General Gaol Delivery, the Exchequer, the Ecclesiastical, the Common Law, the two Deemsters' Courts for the north and south of the island, the Seneschal's Court, the Consistorial, the Licensing, and the High Bailiff's. Each sheading, or subdivision, has its own coroner or sheriff, who can appoint a "lockman" as his deputy; and each parish (there are seventeen) has its own captain and a "sumner," whose duty in old times was to keep order in church and "beat all the doggs." Manx law had, and perhaps to some extent still has, a similar reputation either for allowing criminals in the island to escape easily, or for permitting English criminals to remain unpunished; hence the old ribald verse which represents the Devil singing—

> "That little spot I cannot spare,
> For all my choicest friends are there."

The Deemster's oath is a curiosity in itself:—

ISLAND LAWS. 247

"I do swear that I will execute the laws of the isle justly betwixt party and party as indifferently as the herring's backbone doth lie in the midst of the fish." Formerly the elective House of Keys possessed judicial as well as legislative functions, but this power was taken from it by the Act of 1866. Laws are initiated in the Council and the Tynwald Court, which promulgates them, consists of the members of the Council, and the House of Keys, who unite for the occasion. Tynwald Day as described by Mr. Hall Caine is an interesting, historic, but not an impressive ceremony. A thousand years ago the Norsemen established a form of government on the island, and every fifth of July the Manxman has his open-air Parliament for the promulgation of laws. But it is a gala day rather than a day of business. "Reluctantly I admit," writes Mr. Hall Caine, "that the proceedings were, in themselves, long, tiresome, ineffectual, formless, unimpressive, and unpicturesque. The senior Deemster, the amiable and venerable Sir Wm. Drinkwater, read the titles of the new laws in English. Then the coroner of the premier sheading, Glenfaba, recited the same titles in Manx. Hardly anybody heard them; hardly anybody listened."

The Channel Islands were part of the Duchy of Normandy, and their laws are mostly the ducal customs as set forth in an ancient book known as "Le Grand Coustumier." Acts of the English Parliament do not apply to these Islands unless specifically mentioned, and all causes are determined by their own courts and officers. In Mr. Ansted's standard work on the Channel Islands (revised and edited by E. Toulmin Nicolle, 1893), a long chapter is devoted to the whole subject, and it is so complete and well expressed that I venture without much alteration of phraseology to summarise its leading points. Jersey and Guernsey have diverged greatly from each other in their legal customs, and it is also curious to find that each of the smaller islands possesses its own particular constitutions and courts. The rights and customs of the "States," which are an outcome of the mediæval Royal Court, have constantly undergone modification and have been remodelled, but they retain many of the ancient characteristics. The Bailiff *(Bailli)*, or chief magistrate, is the first civil officer in each island, and usually retains his office for life. He presides at the Royal Court, takes the opinions of the elected Jurats, and when their voices are equal has a casting vote both in civil and criminal cases. The Bailiff is not required either in Jersey or Guernsey to have had a legal education. He is appointed by the Crown, but has usually held some position at the island bar. Formerly the advocates practising in the court of Jersey were nominated by the Bailiff, and were limited to six in number. In 1860, however, the bar was thrown open to every British subject who had been ten years resident in the island, and who was qualified by reason of being a member of the English bar, having taken a law degree at a French University, and having passed an examination in the island. In Guernsey the advocates are also notaries, and frequently hold agencies. The judicial and legislative powers in Jersey are to some extent separate, but in Guernsey they are intimately associated—a fact which accounts for much of the difference in custom in the two islands.

The ancient Norman law contained in " Le Grand Coustumier " dates back to the thirteenth century, was badly revised in the time of Queen Elizabeth, and became the Code. Trial by jury was established in 1786, and the laws on the subject have undergone considerable change. There is a committing magistrate, and the trial takes place at the Criminal Assizes of which there are six in the year. The jury numbers twenty-four; if twenty agree, the verdict is taken; if less than twenty the prisoner is set free. Minor offences are referred to a court of Correctional Police presided over by a magistrate who is independent of the Royal Court. The same magistrate presides over the court for the recovery of small debts, and there is no appeal from his decision. Then there are subsidiary courts for various police purposes, while the Court of Héritage entertains suits regarding real estate. The arbitrary operation of these Courts may have very evil results, especially for strangers who are unlearned in the peculiarities of Jersey law. I find a striking example of this in a magazine of June 15th, 1861, in which a hard experience is detailed with comments which appear to be fully justified by the circumstances. The writer says:—

"Before leaving England I had had a serious quarrel with a former friend and medical attendant, and no long time elapsed after our arrival in the island, before this gentleman sent me in a bill of monstrous proportions—a true 'compte d'apothecaire' as the French express it. At that time I was quite ignorant of the singular con-

ISLAND LAWS. 251

stitution of Jersey law, and how it placed me in the power of any man who chose to sue me whether I owed him money or not. I wrote to the doctor, refusing to pay the full amount of his claim, and referring him to a solicitor in London. He was, however, better acquainted with the Jersey law than myself, as the result will show. Here, before proceeding with my story, I will enter into some explanation of the law of debtor and creditor as it exists in Jersey. This law enables the creditor to enforce his demands summarily, depriving the party sued of his liberty, and leaving him in gaol till the costs of his imprisonment have swelled the amount to be paid : and further, supposing the defendant ultimately gains his suit, and proves his non-liability, no damages for false imprisonment are obtainable. The law leaves him no remedy, for the plaintiff makes no affidavit; and a simple letter from England, requesting a Jersey advocate to enforce payment of a claim, is enough to cast the defendant at once into prison, prior to any judicial investigation into the merits of his case.

"Thus, in Jersey, every man (unless he be a landed proprietor) is at the mercy of every other man, both in the island and out of it. In short, one man can arrest another simply by drawing up an imaginary account on a common bit of paper, and handing it to the nearest lawyer, who will send his clerk with the sheriff's man and imprison the unfortunate victim in default of immediate payment. What is worse still, an arrest can be carried into effect, by means of a simple letter sent through the post. The exception in favour of land-owners of course includes the owners of house property, an exception which mostly benefits Jersey-men, as few but natives possess property in the island. It is only a proprietor who must be sued *before* he can be imprisoned. If the Jersey laws confined the persons merely of strangers sued by the inhabitants of the island, in the arbitrary manner described, the justice of such a practice might still be defended on the plea of preventing them from leaving the island; but no excuse can be found when the Jersey law is made an instrument in the hands of strangers, living out of the jurisdiction of the island, and when it is used to enforce payment of debts incurred in another place, and in which no inhabitant of the island is interested, and when (as sometimes happens) it is employed as a means of extortion. In the first case it can be urged that,

ISLAND LAWS. 253

at least, it gives protection to the islander, which may be all proper enough, though the system is liable to abuse. In the second, the injustice and folly of the law is flagrant. By what right or reason ought the Jersey code, without previous inquiry, to deprive one man of his liberty at the demand of another, when both are strangers, and when the dispute relates to matters wholly beyond its pale, and in reference to which it has no means of obtaining information on oath? Yet such is the case, and thus the Jersey law is converted into a mere tool of iniquity and oppression. In speaking of this strange anomaly in Jersey law, I am not referring to bills of exchange, or to securities of any sort, but merely to simple debts, free from any acknowledgment or signature whatever. In any other Court, such claims would not be entertained for a moment. Surely the law is barbarous enough for the people of Jersey, without its consequences being extended beyond its circumference. But, as matters stand at present, the case stands thus : A and B fall out together. Now B is a rogue. They go to law together, and B demands of A more than he is entitled to. The courts in England are about to decide upon the merits of the case. Meanwhile

B learns that A is gone to Jersey for a short time on business, perhaps connected with this very affair, such, for instance, as looking up an important witness. What does B do? He immediately sends off a letter enclosing his little account to a Jersey lawyer, instructing him to demand payment or lock up A forthwith. The lawyer obeys, of course; A storms—protests—all in vain. He is incarcerated, and is told he may explain as much as he likes afterwards; but, in the meantime, must go to prison, or *pay*. At last poor A, whose liberty is important to him, wearied with the delays which it is the interest of the Jersey lawyers to raise in his suit for judgment, pays the demand into court (au greffe) to be adjudicated on—costs of law, costs of imprisonment and all. The latter item includes 10s. every time the prison door is opened to let him pass on his way to court—a journey he has too often to perform without much approach to a *dénoûment*, and whither he is obliged to go under escort like a criminal; and this process is repeated several times, without the cause even being called on for hearing. Worst of all, when A comes out, he has to decide upon the merits of the case. Meanwhile no remedy against B, who, of course, being satisfied, withdraws his suit at home."

Another seeming anomalous process may be cited. An appeal lies from some of the small Courts to the full Court, or *Nombre Supérieur*, but the jurats who sit in the Court of First Instance are not debarred from sitting in the Full Court when an appeal from their own judgment is being heard! All the proceedings are carried on in the French language, which is again extremely inconvenient for the English residents. The Bailiff comments on the evidence and on the arguments of the pleaders, collects the opinion of the jurats, and delivers judgment. In Guernsey the decisions are given in private. "Pleadings in these courts are very simple," says Mr. Ansted. "The plaintiff must serve on the defendant a summons or declaration, setting forth the nature of his claim, and in some cases the reasons on which it is grounded are added. If not sufficiently definite the declaration is sent back by the Court for amendment. If the defendant means to plead any objections by way of demurrer or special plea, these are at once heard and disposed of. If the parties join issue on the merits of the case, the Court hears the parties, or their counsel, and decides. If the case be intricate the parties are sometimes sent before the Greffier—in Guernsey before one of the jurats,—who reports, condensing the matter in dispute, and presenting the points to the court for decision." Trial by jury does not exist in Guernsey. The court at Alderney is subordinate to that of Guernsey. The jurisdiction in matters of correctional police is final where the offence can be punished by a month's imprisonment or a fine not exceeding £5; otherwise it is referred to Guernsey for trial. The Court of Sark, which has undergone many strange vicissitudes since its institution in 1579, consists of the seneschal, or judge, the prévôt and the greffier, all appointed by the feudal lord, or seigneur. The seneschal is an absolute authority in small cases, but his right of punishment is limited to the narrow bounds of inflicting a fine of about four shillings, and of sentencing to three days' imprisonment. All cases demanding severer treatment are relegated to the Guernsey Courts. Enough has been said to show that Mr. Ansted was justified in declaring that though the islanders were unfitted by their habits and education for any radical change in their peculiar institutions, yet "the practice of the law courts both in Jersey and Guernsey has long been felt to be in many cases cumbrous, not to say objectionable. Indeed, where so much

ISLAND LAWS. 257

that is personal interferes in the administration of justice, and where personal and family influence cannot but be felt, it is not astonishing that reasonable complaints are sometimes heard." Three times during the present century Royal Commissions have enquired into Jersey law, but their recommendations have been systematically ignored. No remedies have been carried out, and the islanders cling with extraordinary pertinacity to customs which are notoriously abused and to priveleges which are opposed to fair-dealing. The Channel Islands and the Isle of Man are standing evidence of the danger incurred by such independence of legal authority as they have hitherto been permitted to enjoy.

The Little Inns of Court.

THE origin of the decadent institutions located in certain grim and dreary-looking piles of building dotting the district of the Inns of Court proper, and known as the little Inns of Court, is involved in considerable obscurity. They appear to have originally held a similar position to the great seats of legal education as the halls of Oxford and Cambridge do to the Universities. But at the present time their relation to the Inns of Court proper is not very clear, and the uses they serve, otherwise than as residential chambers, are just as hard to discover. This state of mistiness concerning them has existed so long that no one now seems to know anything about them, and the evidence taken more than forty years ago by a Royal Commission did so little to clear away the dust and cobwebs hanging about them that they still remain, in the words of Lord Dundreary, "things that no fellow can understand."

Lyon's Inn has since that time been swept

away to make room for the new Courts of Law, without any person evincing the smallest interest in its fate. Concerning this institution all that could be learned by the Royal Commission was contained in the evidence of Timothy Tyrrell, who "believed" that it consisted of members or "ancients," he could not say which; he believed the terms were synonymous. There were then only himself and one other, and within his recollection there had never been more than five, and they had nothing to do beyond receiving the rents of the chambers. There were no students, and the only payment made on account of legal instruction was a sum of £7 13s. 4d. paid to the society of the Inner Temple for a reader; but there had been no reader since 1832. He had heard his father say that the reader "burlesqued the things so greatly" that the ancients were disgusted, and would not have another. There was a hall, but it was used only by a debating society; and there was a kitchen attached to it, but he had never heard of a library.

New Inn appears to have been somewhat more alive than Lyon's, though it does not seem to have done any more to advance the cause of legal education. The property is held under the society of the Middle Temple, by a lease of three hundred years from 1744, at a rent of four pounds a year. Among the stipulations of the lease is one allowing the lessors to hold lectures in the hall, but none had been held since 1846, in consequence, it was believed, of the Middle Temple ceasing to send a reader. The lectures never numbered more than five or six in a year; and there is now no provision of any kind for legal education. Samuel Brown Jackson, who represented the inn before the Royal Commission, said he knew nothing concerning any ancient deeds or documents that would throw any light on the original constitution and functions of the body. If any there were, he "supposed" they were in the custody of the treasurer. The only source of income was the rents of chambers, which then amounted to between eighteen and nineteen hundred pounds a year; and the ancients have no duties beyond the administration of the funds.

Concerning the origin of Clement's Inn, Thomas Gregory, the steward of the society, was unable to afford full information, but he had seen papers dating back to 1677, when there was a conveyance by Lord Clare to one Killett, followed by a Chancery suit between the latter and the principal and ancients of the society, which resulted in a decree under which the property so conveyed became vested in the inn. Some of the papers relating to the inn had been lost by fire, and "some of them," said the witness, "we can't read." The inn, he believed, was formerly a monastery, and took its name from St. Clement. It had once been in connection with the Inner Temple, but he could find no papers showing what were the relations between the two societies, "except," he added, "that a reader comes once a term, but that was dropped for twenty years—I think till about two or three years ago, and then we applied to them ourselves, and they knew nothing at all about it; the under-treasurer said he did not know anything about the reader, and had forgotten all about it." It was the custom for the Inner Temple to submit three names to the ancients; and, said the witness, "we chose one; but then they said that the gentleman was out of town, or away, and that there was no time to appoint another." But no great loss seems to have resulted thereby to the cause of legal education, for it appears that all a reader had ever done was to explain some recent

Act of Parliament to the ancients and commoners, there being no students. The inn had no library and no chapel, but as a substitute for the latter had three pews in the neighbouring church of St. Clement, and also a vault, in which, said the witness, "the principals or ancients may be buried if they wish it."

Some remarkable evidence was given concerning Staples Inn, and the more remarkable for being given by Edward Rowland Pickering, the author of a book on the subject, which publication one of the Commissioners had before him while the witness was under examination. " You state here," said the Commissioner, " that in the reign of Henry V., or before, the society probably became an Inn of Chancery, and that it is a society still possessing the manuscripts of its orders and constitutions." " I am afraid," replied the witness, "that the manuscript is lost. The principal has a set of chambers which were burnt down, and his servant and two children were burnt to death, seventy years ago ; and I rather think that these manuscripts might be lost." Where the learned historian of the inn had obtained the materials for that work is a question which he does not appear to have been in a position to answer; for when asked whether he knew of any trace of a connection between the society and an Inn of Court, he replied, "Certainly, I should say not. It is sixty years since I was there, boy and all." A very strange answer considering the statement in his book. During the sixty years he had been connected or acquainted with the society, he had never heard of the existence of a reader, or of any association of the inn with legal education or legal pursuits. The only connection claimed for the inn by the principal, Andrew Snape Thorndike, was that, when a serjeant was called from Gray's Inn, that society invited the members of Staples Inn to breakfast. There is a singular provision respecting the tenure of chambers in this inn by the ancients. "A person," said this witness, "holds them for his own life, and though he may be seventy years of age, if he can come into the hall, he may surrender them to a very young man, and if that young man should live he may surrender them again at the same age." If a surrender is not made, the chambers revert to the society.

Barnard's Inn is a very old one, and the property has been held on lease from the dean and chapter of Lincoln for more than three hundred years. The society consists of a principal, nine ancients, and five companions, which latter are chosen by the ancients; but we fail to gather from the evidence of Charles Edward Hunt, treasurer and secretary of the inn, by what principles the ancients are guided in the selection. We learn, however, that applications for admission by solicitors are not allowed. Such a thing had occurred once, but it was as long ago as 1827, and "of course," said the witness, "we refused him, and he applied to the court, and after some difficulty he got a rule *nisi* for a mandamus. It came on to be tried before Lord Tenterden, and Lord Tenterden said it could not be granted; that we were a voluntary association, and the court had no jurisdiction." The applicant seems to have based his claim on the ground that Barnard's was an Inn of Chancery, and that, as a solicitor, he had a right to be admitted. The matter was scarcely worth contention, as the privileges of the companions are confined to dining in hall and the chance of being made an ancient, that favoured grade being entitled to "their dinners and some little fees." The books of the society showed no trace of there ever

THE LITTLE INNS OF COURT.   265

having been any students of law connected with the inn. "The oldest thing I find," said the witness, "is that a reader came occasionally from Gray's Inn to read; but what he read about, or who paid him, there is no minute whatever." He did not know when a reader last came from Gray's Inn; he thought it was about two hundred years ago. It only remains to be told of Barnard's Inn that it has not even a library; there had been a few books at one time, the witness told the Commission, but they were sold as useless!

Concerning the remaining little inns—Clifford's, Symond's, and Furnival's—no evidence was taken. They appear to be merely residential chambers, much the same as some of those concerning which we have information in the report of the Royal Commission and the evidence given before it, and the chambers are far from being used exclusively by members of the legal profession. Nearly sixty years ago the present writer found a retired army officer occupying chambers in Clifford's, and on a later occasion made at Symond's Inn, the acquaintance of a curate who resided there with his wife and a young family! Concerning Furnival's Inn, it was incidentally stated by

Michael Doyle, who represented Lincoln's Inn before the Royal Commission, that the latter society received £576 a year under a lease of the former property granted to the late Henry Peto for ninety-nine years, £500 being for rent, and the remainder in lieu of land tax. The witness was, however, unable to give any information as to the manner in which, or the date when, the property was acquired by Lincoln's Inn.

The inquiry by the Royal Commission resulted in the recommendation of some very important changes in the constitution of the little Inns of Court and the administration of the several properties; but these, we learn, have been modified so much in their adoption as to have been of very little value. The societies have long outlived the purposes for which they were instituted, though their principals and officials seem to attach considerable importance to their continued existence. It is probable, however, that their *raison d'étre* being gone, they will all sooner or later go the way of Lyon's Inn, and become things of the past.

Obiter.

By George Neilson.

THE claims of the legal profession to culture were cleverly belittled by Burns, when he made the New Brig of Ayr wax sarcastic over the town councillors of the burgh :—

> "Men wha grew wise priggin owre hops an' raisins,
> Or gather'd lib'ral views in Bonds and Seisins."

Bonds and seisins are certainly not the happiest intellectual feeding ground. "I assure you," said John Riddell, a great peerage antiquary, "that to spend one's time in seeking for a name or a date in a bit of crabbed old writing does not improve the reasoning powers." Riddell was a keen critic of Cosmo Innes, who subsequently had the happiness of passing the comment upon Riddell's observation that "perhaps it is not in *reasoning* that Mr. Riddell excels." Yet the annals of the law shew many splendid examples of the union of close textual study of manuscript, with an enlarged outlook on first principles and with keen critical insight. Perhaps Madox was a more permanently serviceable scholar than Selden. One can see from Coke's margins, his infinite superiority to Bacon in exact knowledge at first hand of older English law. But when all is said, we could have done much better without Coke and Madox than without Bacon or Selden. It is delightful to be able to appeal to Chaucer for perhaps the most emphatic compliment to law, in respect to its capacity for literature, that it has ever received. Amongst all the Canterbury pilgrims, there was no weightier personage than the Man of Law :—

> "Nowher so bisy a man as he ther nas,
> And yet he semed bisier than he was.
> In termes hadde he caas and domes alle
> That from the tyme of King William were falle,
> Therto he coude endyte and make a thing
> Ther could no wight pinche at his wryting,
> And every statut coude he pleyn by rote."

Yet it was this learned and successful counsel, alone of the party, who knew the poet's works through and through, and had the list of them at his finger-ends. Good Master Chaucer for this touch we offer hearty thanks! Was it in Herrick's mind when he penned his fine tribute to Selden ?

> "I, who have favoured many, come to be
> Graced, now at last, or glorified by thee."

. . . .

Wits and poets have had many hard things to say in jest and in earnest about the legal profession and its work. Herrick bracketed law and lawyers with diseases and doctors, in a fashion hinting that the relation of cause and effect existed between both pairs ;—

> "As many laws and lawyers do express,
> Nought but a kingdom's ill-affectedness.
> Even so those streets and houses do but show
> Store of diseases where physicians flow."

. . . .

It was an old story this linking of the practitioners of law and medicine in one yoke of abuse. The reason given for both categories in early satire is sufficiently curious. It was because they took fees! Walter Map declared the Cistercian creed to be that no man could serve God without mammon. Ancient satire equally objected to the service of man, either legally or medically, under these conditions. "The Romaunt of the Rose" has the traditional refrain of other strictures in verse, when it declares that

> "Physiciens and advocates,
> Gon right by the same yates,   *yates, gates*
> They selle hir science for winning.   *winning, gain*
>
> . . . .
>
> For they nil in no maner gree   *no kind of good will*
> Do right nought for charitee,"

The same idea, precisely, finds voice in the poem attributed to Walter Map, wherein the doctor and the lawyer come together under the lash, because no hope can be based upon either of them unless there be money in the case. "But if the marvellous man see coin, the very worst disease is quite curable, the very falsest cause just, praiseworthy, pious, true, and pleasing to God." Perhaps these ancient sarcasms were keener on the leech than the lawyer. "The Romaunt of the Rose" goes so far as to say that if the physicians had their way of it,

> "Everiche man shulde be seke,
> And though they dye, they set not a leke
> After: whan they the gold have take
> Ful litel care for hem they make.
> They wolde that fourty were seke at onis!
> Ye, two hundred in flesh and bonis!
> And yit two thousand as I gesse
> For to encresen her richesse."

. . . . . .

No doubt the men of medicine would have been much more vulnerable on another line, for it was no satirist but a learned medical professor, Arnauld de Villeneuve, who, in the beginning of the fourteenth century, advised his students as follows:—"The seventh precaution," said he, "is of a general application. Suppose that you cannot understand the case of your patient, say to him with assurance that he hath an obstruction of the liver." No legal professor surely was ever guilty of the indiscretion of *saying* such a thing as this!

. . . .

The ineradicable public prejudice against legal charges as flagrantly exorbitant is only a modified form of an older idea exemplified above that lawyers should have no fees at all. And as to this day the plain man has never fully reconciled himself to the doctrine that the lawyer is only an agent, and not called upon to sit in the first instance in judgment on his client, so in the past the professional defence of a criminal appeared a very venal transaction.

> "Thow I have a man i-slawe,
> And forfetyd the kynges lawe
> I sal fyndyn a man of lawe
> Wyl takyn myn peny and let me goo."

. . . .

How reprehensible a thing to take fees was long reckoned admits of curious illustration. "Before the end of the thirteenth century," says that never-failing authority, Pollock and Maitland's "History of English Law," there already exists a legal profession, a class of men who make money by representing litigants before the courts and by giving legal advice. The evolution of this class has been slow, for it has been withstood by certain ancient principles." Amongst these retarding influences lay the half-religious scruple about the propriety of payment—men as usual swallowing the camel first and straining at the gnat afterwards. Of course the subject had to be illuminated by monkish tales and death-bed repentances. There was, according to the Carlisle friar who penned the "The Chronicle of Lanercost,"—writing under the year 1288,— a young clerk in the diocese of Glasgow, whose mind " was given rather to the court of the rich than to the cure of souls. He was called Adam Urri, and was laically learned in the laic laws, disregarding the commands of God against the Praecorialia [so in the printed text, but, query, Praetorialia?] of Ulpian. He used the statutes of the Emperor in litigating causes, for payment of money. But when he had grown old and famous in this his wickedness, and was striving by his astuteness to entangle the affairs of a poor little widow, the divine mercy laid hold on him, assailing his body with sudden infirmity, and bringing his mind to plead (*enarraret*) more for another life." Condemning utterly the lawyer's court, he turned over a new leaf, predicted the day of his own death, and died punctually conform to the phophecy, leaving an example unctuously used by the friar to teach future generations "how wide was the gulf betwixt the service of God and the vanity of this world." We shall not be far wrong in regarding, as of more historic interest, the indication of the immorality of fees, and the important reference to Ulpian as an authority in the *forum causidicorum* of thirteenth century Scotland.

. . . .

Amongst the amiable conceptions of the middle age was the notion that the Evil One often manifested a particular zeal against sin. He was regarded with a different eye from that with which we regard him, and he rewarded faith with actual appearances such as only spiritualists can now-a-days command. Some of them were not very engaging, however praiseworthy may have been their object and occasion. Simeon of Durham, an eminently respectable contemporary author, wrote of the death of King William Rufus in the year 1100 that the popular voice considered the wandering flight of Tyrell's arrow a token of the "virtue and vengeance of God." And he added that about that time the Devil had frequently shewn himself in the woods "and no wonder, because in those days law and justice were all but silent." The logic of this *because,* not apparent on the surface, becomes less obscure when it is remembered that in the mediæval devil the character of Arch-Enemy is so much subordinated to that of Arch-Avenger.

. . . .

The direct relation of not only the Saints but of the Deity itself to human affairs was a conception so clear to the mediæval mind that it saw nothing irreverent in a title deed being taken in the Supreme name, or in marshalling "*Deus Omnipotens*" at the head of the list of witnesses to a charter. This anthropomorphic practice gave occasion to one of the sharpest of Walter Map's jokes against the Cistercians. Three abbots of that order petitioning on behalf of one of their number and his abbey for the restoration of certain lands by King Henry II. as having been injuriously taken away from the claimant's abbey, represented to the King in his court that for God's sake he ought to cause the lands to be restored and they assured him and gave him God himself as their guarantor *(fidejussorem)* that if he did, God would greatly increase his honour upon earth. King Henry found it difficult to resist the appeal thus made to him but called the Archdeacon Walter Map to advise. This he did well-knowing that this counsellor did not love the Cistercians, and that he might thus find a creditable way out of a tight corner. The Archdeacon was equal to the occasion. "My lord," said he to the King, "they offer you a guarantor; you should hear their guarantor speak for himself." "By the eyes of God," replied Henry, "it is just and conform to reason that guarantors themselves should be heard upon the matter of their guarantee." Then rising with a gentle smile (not a grin, expressly says Giraldus Cambrensis) the shrewd monarch retired leaving the disappointed abbots covered with confusion.

. . . .

Of the many ties between literature and law, one, not by any means the least interesting on the list, is the quantity of legal citations, phrases, metaphors and analogies which got swept into the wide nets of the poets. Amongst such scraps there are few so successful and still fewer so pathetic as one in which a metrical historian, drawing near the close, both of his days and his chronicle, figured himself as summoned on short *induciæ* at the instance of Old Age to appear at a court to answer serious charges, where no help was for him save through grace and the Virgin as his advocate.

Elde me maistreis wyth hir brevis,	*elde, age*
Ilke day me sare aggrevis,	*brevis, writ*
Scho has me maid monitioune	*ilke, each*
To se for a conclusioune	*quhilk, which*
The quhilk behovis to be of det ;	*of det, of right*
Quhat term of tyme of that be set	
I can wyt it be na way,	*wyt, know*
Bot weill I wate on schort delay	
At a court I mon appeire	
Fell accusationis thare til here	
Quhare na help thare is bot grace.	*bot, without*
The maikless Madyn mon purchace	*maikless, matchless*
That help ; and to sauff my state	*purchace, procure*
I haiff maid hir my advocate.	*sauff, save*

Androw of Wyntoun's verse it must be owned was verse on the plane of a notary public, and oft the common form of legal writ supplied sorrily enough the deficiencies of his imagination. But here for once the simple dignity of the thought bore him up and carried him through.

Index.

Aberdeen, gipsies at, 175
Abjuring the realm, 15
Abjuration, 69
Abolishing right of Sanctuary, 16
Adultery, penalty of, 11
Africa, ordeal in, 24-25
Amphitheatre, sports of, 112
An eye for an eye, 137
Ancient tenures, 95-108
Andrews, William, Cock-Fighting, 196-200
Anglo-Saxon Church, 14
Aram, Eugene, 212
Ashford, Mary, 40-41
Asyla in Greece, 14
Axon, W. E. A., Sanctuaries, 13-22; Laws relating to the Gipsies, 165-178

Babylonia, law of, 3-4
Balance, ordeal of, 27
Barbarous Punisements, 132-148
Barnard's Inn, 263
Beetles, trial of, 157
Begbie, William, murder of, 210
Beverley, Sanctuary at, 19-20
Bible Law, 1-12
Bible, ordeal of the, 37
Bible, weighing against, 27
Bier, ordeal of, 36
Bird, Robert, Cockieleerie Law, 200-204
Biretta, 53
Black Book of Hereford, 101
Black Parliament, 225
Blood, laws written in, 135; stains, 222
Boiling to death, 135
Book of Common Prayer, abolished, 194
Borough English, 104-106
Breaking straws, 48; rods, 49
Buccleuch, Barons of, 107
Bull relating to English Sanctuaries, 15

Bull, trial of, 150
Burned alive, 134
Burgess, S., Bible Law, 1-12

Canning, Elizabeth, 172-173
Canon Law, 187, 225
Castles, a centre of power, 74
Cattle stealing, 74
Channel Islands, Laws of the, 242-243, 248-257
Charges, prejudice against, 271
Charles I., Trial of, 182
Chaucer's compliment to the law, 268
Cheltenham, Manor of, 94
Chemical test, 220
Christians, early punishment of, 137
Church and ordeals, 29
Clarke, Sidney W., Barbarous Punishments, 132-144
Clement's Inn, 260
Cock-Fighting in Scotland, 196-204
Cockieleerie Law, 200-204
Cock, tried for laying an egg, 154
Commonwealth Law and Lawyers, 178-196
Continental Feudalism, 77-82
Conveyancing Symbols, 50-51
Copyhold, 49, 83
Corsnedd, ordeal of, 35
Commandments, breaking, 3
Cross, ordeal of the 33
Crown, 56
Coventry Acts, 142-143
Court Baron, 84
Customary Court, 84
Crucifixion, 136

Dead bodies brought to place of judgment, 232
Debts, limitation of, 9
Declining knighthood, 63-64

INDEX.

Defilement, 8
Delivery of turf or twig, 50
Deposition of kings, 56
Devices of the Sixteenth Century Debtors, 161-164
Divine right of kings, 193
Dog carrying, 140
Dogs in recognition of tenure, 101
Dream evidence, 214-217
Dudley lands, 64
Durham Sanctuary, 17, 19

Escheats, 226
Emma, Queen, tried by ordeal, 30
Englishry, law of, 70
Executing gipsies, 167, 170

Failure to extripate gipsies from England, 170
Fatal Links, 205-223
Father, powers of, 9
Ferocity of forest laws, 119,
Feudal lord, powers of the, 64
Feudal system, 58-62
Fining jurymen, 124
Fire ordeal, 28
Flagellation, 61
Flags, rendering for tenure, 101
Forests, great, 115-116
Forgery, punishments, 142
Fortune telling, 169
France, penal laws of, 140-141; Trials of animals in, 149-154
Frankalmoign, 103
Free alms, 103-104
Fridstools, 17, 20
Frost, Thomas, Trial by jury in Old Times, 122-131; Trials of animals, 149-160; Little Inns of Court, 258-266
Furnival's Inn, 265

Gavelkind 106-107
Ghosts, 217-220
Gibbet, gipsy rescued from, 176
Gipsies, laws relating to the, 165-178
Glove, 92
Godiva story, 74
Grand Serjeantry, 100
Great Civil War, 179
Greenacre case, 209,

Hampden, John, 182
Hanged, drawn, and quartered, 133-134
Hasp and staple symbol, 52-53
Hat as a symbol, 53-54
Hawaii, ordeals in, 25
Henry VIII., laws against gipsies, 169
Hereford Fair, 101
Heresy, 228
Heriots, 91-92
Herrick on lawyers, 269
High treason, trial for, 122-124; punishments for, 132-135
Hindoos, ordeals of the, 26-27
Holzmann, Maria Ann, murder of, 206-209
Homage, 53
Homicide, 11
Horse, trial of, 151
Hot iron, ordeal of, 27, 30, 31, 32
Howlett, England, the Manor and Manor Law, 83-94; Ancient Tenures, 95-108
Hugh of Avalon, 120

Ignorance, sin of, 7
Iniquities, legal, 145
Irish Island Laws, 238-239
Isle of Man, Laws of the, 243-247
Island Laws, 237-257

Jews, extortions of, 73
Jocular tenure, 102

King's power limited, 12
Knight, service of, 96

Lanercost, the chronicle of, 272
Law under the Feudal System, 58-82
Law and Medicine abused, 269-270
Laws of the Forest, 109-121
Laws relating to the Gipsies, 165-178
Left-handed murder, 214
Letters of IV. Forms, 163
Lesemajesty, crimes of, 229-231
Lincoln's Inn, 266
Lipski, 213
Literature and Law, 275
Little Inns of Court, 258-266
Lords, power of, 58

INDEX. 279

Lord Chief Justice Popham, stolen by gipsies, 170
Loss of right hand, 138
Lyon's Inn, 259

Macdonald, James C., Devices of the Sixteenth Century Debtors, 161-164
Magna Charta, 63, 98
Manchester, Sanctuary at, 15, 16, 17
Manor and Manor Law, 83-94
Manor, origin of, 88
Marriage in feudal times, 59
Marriage laws, altering, 195
Marrying to atone for violence, 64
Martin, Maria, 214
Middle Ages, ordeals of, 29
Military service, 59
Military punishments, 136
Money raised by marriage, 72
Mortal Combat, 37-41
Mosaic law, 3
Mutilation, a favourite mode of punishment, 141-144
Muswell Hill murder, 213

Neilson, George, on Symbols, 43-57; Post Mortem Trials, 224-236; Obiter, 267-276
New Inn, 259
New way of paying old debts, 163
Nimrod, 111
Norman forest laws, 117

Oath, refusal to bear witness of, 8; of fealty, 60
On Symbols, 43-57
Oppression of gipsies under Queen Elizabeth, 171
Ordeals, 24-42

Palace regulations, 138-140
Parricide, punishment for, 137
Paul's Cross, preaching at, 194
Peacock, Edward, Laws of the Forest, 109-121; Commonwealth Law and Lawyers, 179-196
Peine forte et dure, 145-148
Penal Code, English, 145
Penn and Mead, trial of, 125

Persecution of gipsies, 171
Plantations, gipsies sent to, 178
Plays acted by gipsies, 176
Pigs, trial of, 150, 151, 152, 153, 157
Pillory, 142, 144
Poison, 135, 138
Poison, ordeal, 28
Poisoning, punishment for, 135
Poor laws, 9
Post-Mortem Trials, 224-236
Prejudice against gipsies, 172
Protecting the church in war time, 102-103
Proverb, oldest, 111
Punishments under Saxons, 61

Quakers, trial of, 125-131

Rann, Ernest H., trials in superstitious ages, 22-42; Fatal Links, 205-223
Reasoning power, 267
Rebel Heads on City gates, 134
Refuge, cities of, 14
Regicides, 134
Robbing travellers in feudal times, 73-74
Robert de Belesone, cruel acts of, 65
Robert the Bruce, Conspiracy, 225
Rod in Scotland, 49
Roman Empire in its glory, 114
Rose Tenures, 102
Ruskin, Jno., on Cœur de Lion, 72

Sacrifice, laws relating to, 5-7
Sacrilege, 8
Sanctuaries, 13-22
Scilly Islands, laws of the, 239
Scoggan, Queen's jester, 163-164
Scotch Islands, laws of the, 239-242
Scotland, sanctuaries of, 21-22
Scott, John, of Edinburgh, 161-163
Scutage, 98
Self-slaughter, 229
Ship-money tax, 181
Shaving the head for theft, 69
Siamese, ordeals of the, 26
Silver spear, 55

INDEX.

Slavery, discharge from, 45
Slaves, ill treatment of, 8, 10 ;
   under the Saxons, 60
Slaying gipsies, 175-176
Sods offered at the altar, 48
Spindle on the altar, 51
Staff and baton, 50
Staples Inn, 262
Star Chamber, 124-125
Strangulation, punishment by,
Straws, breaking, 48
Stocks, 67
Switzerland, trials of animals in, 154
Symond's Inn, 265

Thornton, Abraham, 40-41
Towns amerced, 70
Traitors, exempted from the Sanctuary, 15
Treason, trials for, 233
Trial by Jury in old times, 122-131
Trials of Animals, 149-160
Trials in superstitious ages, 22-42
Tynwald Day, 247

Usury, law of, 9

Villeinage, 86
Violating the sanctuary, 14, 21

Wager of Battel, 37, 41
Walters, Cuming, Law under the Feudal system, 58-82 ; Island Laws, 237-257
Wand, 49
Welcoming gipsies to England, 168
Westminster, sanctuary of, 20
Whipping 61 ; Post 67
William I., Forest Laws of, 118 ; Burial of, 225
William the Red, Forest laws of, 119
Witchcraft, 144-45
Wollen Industry, protection of, 144
Women, free bench of, 93
Working of the sanctuary system, 16, 17

www.ingramcontent.com/pod-product-compliance
Lightning Source LLC
Chambersburg PA
CBHW020732180526
45163CB00001B/204